Crimes and

MisDumbMeanors

Published in Nashville, Tennessee, by Rutledge Hill Press®, 211 Seventh Avenue North, Nashville, Tennessee 37219.
Distributed in Canada by H. B. Fenn & Company, Ltd., 34 Nixon Road, Bolton, Ontario L7E 1W2.
Distributed in Australia by The Five Mile Press Pty., Ltd., 22 Summit Road, Noble Park, Victoria 3174.
Distributed in New Zealand by Tandem Press, 2 Rugby Road, Birkenhead, Auckland 10.
Distributed in the United Kingdom by Verulam Publishing, Ltd., 152a Park Street Lane, Park Street, St. Albans, Hertfordshire AL2 2AU.

Typography by E. T. Lowe Publishing Company

ISBN: 1-55853-673-6

Library of Congress Cataloging-in-Publication Data is available.

Printed in the United States of America

1 2 3 4 5 6 7 8 9—02 01 00 99 98

This book is dedicated to the people in our books who, like us, have made some bad mistakes and poor choices in their lives. And to the good Lord for giving second chances and the wisdom to learn from our mistakes.

Acknowledgments

We want to extend a personal thank-you to all of the wonderful officers and law-enforcement personnel who took the time to share their stories with us.

Also, a special thank-you to the hundreds of radio personalities, their producers, and listeners across the country for allowing us to entertain them.

There are two special people we'd like to thank for all their help. They are our publicist Natasha Mink and our editor Mike Towle. They worked many long and hard hours to make these books possible, going above and beyond the call of duty. Thank you both so much.

Introduction

Three years ago we sat down in a coffee shop and came up with a list of twenty-five different topics for a book. The list included everything from psychic pets and puzzles, to great American ranches and circus freaks. *America's Dumbest Criminals* was not our first choice of subjects on the list, but it was the overwhelming favorite of "the Powers That Be." It wasn't until we finally went out on the road and met the people who read our first book that we realized why this was the series of books we were meant to write.

A bookstore manager in Oklahoma told us about an elderly woman who was a regular customer and a devoted fan of ours. One day she came to the manager to ask if we had written another dumb-crime book. The manager explained that we did have another one that was about to be published, but it wasn't out yet. The little old lady explained to the manager why the book was so important to her.

"I finally found a book that my husband really likes," she said. "Every night he reads one story from the book and chuckles to himself. Then he reads the same story out loud to me and we both laugh. He then sets the book on the bedside table and falls asleep. He enjoys those stories so much that he just wants to make them last for as long as he can!"

While at a recent book signing in Jackson, Mississippi, we were approached by a mother and her thirteen-year-old son. She looked very excited. He looked somewhat timid. Mom began with a question we've gotten used to.

"Are you the dumb criminal guys that were on the radio this morning?"

Yes, we are the dumb criminal guys. We've learned to accept this as a compliment and a title.

She went on to say, "We heard you on the way to school, and y'all were so funny that my son, who hates to read, said, 'I'd read that book, Mom.' So we're here to buy all three of your books for him because I'm so excited that he finally wants to read something."

A family in Louisville, Kentucky, told us, "Thank you for bringing laughter back into our house." The smiles on their faces were something we will never forget.

Wonderful moments like these prove one thing. If three guys who have "been there, dumb that" can do something that affects so many people in a positive way, then God really can use anybody to do anything. We're living proof.

Crimes and

MISDUMBMEANORS

Truth *and* Consequences

Some criminals will go to any length to prove their innocence, even if it proves them guilty.

John Jenkins, an Akron, Ohio, police officer, and his partner made a late-night traffic stop in a known drug area. A search of the vehicle turned up two well-used "crack" pipes, and the driver and his passenger were arrested.

Both men vehemently denied the pipes were theirs. The passenger's pipe was found on the floor board on his side of the car, technically, "within his control."

"I'm tellin' you the truth, man, this is not my pipe!" he insisted.

"Well," Jenkins responded, "it was on your side of the car."

"But I swear to you it's not mine," he argued. With that, he removed his left shoe and pulled a pipe from it. "*This* is my crack pipe!"

A Single Thread of Evidence

This story is about three stooges who managed to leave behind a string of evidence connecting them to the crime.

Los Angeles Sheriff's Deputy Charles Cortez responded to a silent alarm at a business on the south side. Cortez noticed broken glass in the alley directly below a window apparently used to gain entry. Shining his flashlight through the window, he could see the entire floor of the sewing shop. His sweeping light landed on an open door on the other side of the room. *Well, I know how they got in and I know how they got out,* he thought to himself. *Now, what'd they get?*

He crept down the alley and turned the corner, where the open door stood. Just then a backup unit pulled up.

"Think they're still in there?" an officer asked.

"No, they're long gone by now," Cortez responded, shining his light up and down the open door.

"The owner's on his way down to see what's missin'," the backup informed him.

Deputy Cortez smiled. "I know what's missin'. A sewing machine. One of those big industrial jobs."

"How do you know that?" the puzzled officer asked.

"Look down here."

Inside the circle of light lay a thread—a heavy duty industrial thread. Its loose end had hooked itself on the rough wooden floor. Officer Cortez began to follow the thread . . . out the door . . . down the alley . . . across the street . . . up another alley. Then through a backyard, up some steps, and under a door. He radioed for assistance.

With policemen surrounding the house, Cortez knocked on the door. It flew open just long enough for the occupant to slam it shut. Officers stormed the house, past the stolen sewing machine in the kitchen. The three men inside were arrested and charged with breaking and entering, burglary, and possession of stolen property.

Caught by a single thread of evidence. Some people can be sew dumb.

A Lifer Turned Do-It-Yourselfer

3

Out of Cambridge, Massachusetts, comes the tale of the inmate who had been found guilty of a capital crime, escaped the death penalty, and received a life sentence, although he could not escape "the electric throne."

Inmates with televisions are required to wear headphones while watching the tube so as not to disturb the other inmates. The headphones had to be approved by the prison staff and meet safety requirements. Unfortunately, Laurence Baker, forty-seven, had other ideas. Brainy Baker made his own headphones and was using them without permission one night. He was watching *When Toilets Attack!* in his cell with his nifty homemade headphones on, seated on his deluxe prison toilet. Now, if you've ever seen a prison toilet, you know they are made entirely of stainless steel. Just take our word for it.

Engrossed in the show and still wearing his homemade headphones (which he had wired directly into the back of his television set), Baker was reaching for a necessary toilet accessory when his headphones gave him a little jolt of electricity. Larry jumped, the headphones slipped, and kerplunked into the toilet water. And voila!

Larry had just invented the first combination electric chair-toilet with a personal THX sound system built right in. We believe the late Mr. Baker is the only person who has actually tried this revolutionary device.

 **Jail Bird**

The guy in Woodbury, Minnesota, was a good thief. He'd broken into a pen housing at least a dozen homing pigeons, and had stolen every one.

All had gone smoothly until he sold the birds to a "fence" on the black market. The buyer of the stolen goods was very upset the next day when he discovered that all the pigeons had flown the coop. The homing pigeons had returned to their rightful owner.

Acting on an anonymous tip (wonder who that might've been), the police arrested the young "bird brain."

A Doper Who Came Up a Little Short

After stopping a speeding car driving erratically across the George Washington Bridge one night, Officer John Frank and his partner observed the driver squirming around in his seat as they cautiously approached the car.

They asked the driver to step to the rear of his vehicle. The driver did as he was told, but he looked awfully nervous about it. As he stepped out of the driver's side door, he didn't seemed to straighten up all the way. He walked slowly, hunched over, with his trousers pulled up. He was sticking out his belly as far as he could, apparently trying to hold his pants up. The officers were grinning by the time this geek got to the trunk of his car.

Before Frank and his partner could say a word, the suspect took a breath and his pants slid down. When the guy straightened up ever so slightly, a glass vial slipped out of his pants leg and dropped onto the pavement. The officers stared at the vial and then looked up to see the

21

Then another vial fell. And another and another, until fourteen glass vials lay on the pavement at the man's feet.

suspect staring straight ahead and whistling, as though nothing were out of the ordinary. Then another vial fell. And another and another, until fourteen glass vials lay on the pavement at the man's feet—all filled with crack cocaine.

The pusher in the leaky pants smiled meekly back at the officers.

"I forgot that I wore boxers today," the sheepish dude said.

Which goes to show that briefs can be quite legal, and sure hold contraband better than boxer shorts do.

6 Aliens Stole My Brain!

Years ago the police in the Boston area were having a scanning problem. Specifically, police scanners were in the wrong hands. When the bad guys can listen to everything the good guys say, serving warrants, raiding drug houses, and catching crooks in the act becomes that much harder.

These officers took a cue from Orson Welles and his famous *War of the Worlds* radio broadcast. Only theirs went out over a "police only" frequency.

The dispatchers sent out an alert of a "massive alien invasion over the South Downs." They described huge spaceships and warned of possible annihilation for mankind. Actually, the officers were parked in their cars watching an empty field. Within moments, though, that empty field was filled with strange creatures.

When the police flipped on their headlights, they gasped. Before them were drug dealers, petty crooks, and otherwise law-abiding citizens who were illegally

monitoring police communications on restricted fre-
quencies. The cops confiscated drugs, made arrests, got
people with outstanding warrants, and gave a stern lec-
ture on the use of scanning equipment. But they all had
one chance to "phone home" from the station downtown.

Her Story Stinks, But It Works for Me

Cops have heard it all from speeding motorists, and being lied to every day isn't a lot of fun. The truth can be a refreshing change. A Mississippi state trooper got such a treat one afternoon, "courtesy" of a harried mother of three who had been clocked doing eighty in a thirty-five-mile-an-hour zone.

With the pedal to the metal, the dragster mom was rolling down all of the van's windows as she zigzagged through traffic. When she finally pulled over, an officer approached the driver's window and noticed the kids in back fanning the air with their heads out the open windows—except for one ten-year-old boy in the back, smiling angelically. That's when it hit the officer straight in the nostrils, a sulfurous stench emanating from the minivan and sending the officer staggering backward.

"May I see your driver's license and registration, ma'am?"

"Here, officer, I know I was speeding," the woman

said, holding her nose with one hand while passing her papers over with the other.

The officer took a step back to breathe. "Is there a problem, ma'am?"

"I'll say. My son . . . well, he has . . . gas."

Suddenly, the seven-year-old gasping for air next to the back-seat perpetrator blurted out, "*Jake farted and we couldn't breathe!*"

The mom continued: "I had everybody roll down their windows and sped up to air out the van, officer. I'm sorry."

"*We couldn't breathe!*" the little seven-year-old emphasized.

"Well, I guess that was a life-and-death medical emergency," the trooper said, struggling to keep a straight face. "But next time, just pull over and step out of the vehicle, okay?" He then looked at the ten-year-old still grinning in the back seat, "And Jake, stay away from the beans."

Jake conceded, "I guess it was the burritos, officer. Sorry."

Bloomin' Idiot

Police officers in Citrus Heights, California, responded swiftly to the 911 call. The man on the other end of the line told the dispatcher that he had just captured a thief on his property and was holding him at gunpoint. When police arrived on the scene, they found homeowner Payton Harrison still pointing a .38 caliber revolver at the young man he had just caught trying to steal his property.

"I caught him! I caught him red-handed," Harrison boasted proudly. "This little punk was trying to rip me off, but I was just a little too smart for him."

"Okay, sir," one of the officers said. "You can put the gun away. We'll take it from here."

"No problem, officer," he assured them.

"Is this your house?" an officer asked.

"Yes, it is. I've lived here about a year," he said.

"You want to tell us what's goin' on here?"

"Yeah, sure," the owner replied. "I was doin' some work in the basement, when I happened to look up and see this pair of legs go by the window. Well, my backyard is fenced in, and I'm the only one who lives here, so I know it's got to be somebody who ain't supposed to be here. I grab my .38, slip upstairs, and sneak out the back door. And sure enough, there he is comin' out of the greenhouse with an armload."

"An armload of what?" the cop asked.

"Of marijuana! Can you believe it? This little punk was rippin' off my best pot plants. The evidence is layin' right there by the porch. I want to press charges."

The stunned officer looked at the large pile of plants on the ground and asked the kid, "Is this really what you were stealing, son?"

"Yes, sir," the scared teen admitted.

As the young thief was being escorted to a patrol car by another cop, the officer turned to the man: "Sir, at this time I'm placing you under arrest. Turn around and put your hands behind your back."

"Me?" the dumbfounded felon asked. "What for? I didn't do anything wrong. I'm the one who was gettin' ripped off. I called you!"

"You're under arrest for felony possession of marijuana," the officer informed him.

"You've got to be kiddin' me," the man groaned in disbelief. "I call the cops on a burglar and I end up goin' to jail. This is one of the stupidest things I ever heard of."

The officer nodded at the man. "I couldn't agree with you more."

The Half-Naked Truth

On a cold winter's night in rural Illinois, the brainier folks snuggled under warm covers. One dummy, an armed robber, thought it would be a perfect night to "make some money" at an out-of-the-way tavern with few customers but plenty of cash on hand.

The robber drove out into the cold night, parked his vehicle alongside the tavern, grabbed his shotgun, pulled on a ski mask, and boldly strolled into the tavern. Three minutes later, his business was done.

Moments later, after the bartender had called police, a man walked in wearing only underwear, sat down at the bar, and ordered a cup of coffee. When the state police arrived, the bartender mentioned that the half-naked man looked like the robber. The officer looked over at him. Even if the cool guy was innocent, the officer was curious why anyone would be running around almost naked in twenty-degree weather.

"I lost my clothes playing poker and came here to drown my sorrows."

"I lost my clothes playing poker and came here to drown my sorrows."

"Aliens abducted me and probed me with strange surgical devices."

"A gang jumped me to get my trendy team jacket and expensive sneakers."

The officer patiently waded his way through the stories before the man finally confessed: "The robbery went just like I planned it. Nobody got hurt and nobody could identify me, and then I got back to my car. That's when I realized I had locked the car and left the keys in the ignition."

"But how did you lose your clothes?"

The naked numbnut figured if he started down the road, the police would spot him and question him. But maybe if he deposited his clothes, weapon, and stolen loot in the dumpster near his "getaway" car, he might get away unnoticed. The police found the dummy's clothes, shotgun, and cash right where he said they'd be.

Beeper-to-Beeper Love

People are very attached to their beepers, especially when such devices are suddenly—and illegally—detached from their person.

A young professional in a small New York town was robbed and, among other things, the thief got his beeper. This was no cheapo beeper; this was the deluxe, voicemail-get-the-news-sports-messages-take-out-the-garbage type of beepers that run upwards of forty bucks a month. After two beeperless days of cold turkey, the yuppie called the cops with a plan.

The cops played along. The victim had his sister call the beeper and leave a message for the dumbo: "I really enjoyed meeting you, and I sure hope you're going to call me. My number is 555-7897. This is Rhonda. Call me, cutie." She led him on by saying that if he called in the next half hour, they could meet and have a grand time.

Sure enough, the dummy took the bait and called "Rhonda" back. With the officers calling the shots, she arranged a meeting on a nearby street corner. The thief described what he'd be wearing and hinted he would have a special surprise for her.

Four patrol cars lay in wait with six officers on foot when the taxi approached the corner. Hopping out of the cab was the man wearing the khakis and blue shirt the thief had described over the phone. Before he could introduce himself, the cops had him down, kissing the sidewalk instead of Rhonda.

As it turned out, the stolen beeper was the least of the bungler's problems. His "surprise" was a pound of marijuana in the back seat of the cab, which proves, once again, that with brains, a little creativity, and the right bait, you can catch any dumb criminal, any time.

Stuck in Their Own Stupidity

A couple in Michigan ran a small convenience store near a lake—they did a booming business selling fishing supplies and cold drinks for fishermen's ice chests.

Once they got a call at two in the morning. The store's alarm had been tripped. When the police arrived, they found the front window of the store had been smashed and the store looted. The couple rolled back their surveillance camera tape and watched as the whole scene unfolded on this dumb criminal situation comedy.

It began when a car pulled up to the front door of their store, and two men hopped out. In full view of the cameras, one of the guys picked up a big rock and hefted it through the window. The Terrible Two stepped right into the store. Finding no money in the register, they grabbed some cigarettes and other essentials like beer and bait. While the two dummies scooped up several cartons of cigarettes, they looked right into the camera for a close-up on the surveillance camera. They disappeared as quickly as they had appeared and were nowhere to be found when police arrived at the scene. Until the next morning, that is.

The owner of the market was a little shocked when the crooks walked in the next morning. The two explained that their car was stuck. The owner went with them across the street while his wife called the cops.

It seems Slow and Slower had backed across the road after robbing the store. What they couldn't see in the dark of night was a boat ramp into the lake. Try as they might, they couldn't get their wheels out of the mud. So they walked home and waited for morning to retrieve their car. The market owner kept up the act by offering to call a tow truck, but before he could call, four squad cars and a police tow truck arrived and took care of them—for free.

A Funny Vent

It was 3:00 A.M. when Fort Worth, Texas, Deputy Sheriff Jim Reed answered a call to meet a complainant at his residence. The caller was standing outside waiting for the officer as he pulled up.

They exchanged greetings, and the man commenced telling the officer that, while walking his dog for a nature call, he thought he heard someone yelling for help. It was a quiet, still night, and both men cocked their heads to listen. Sure enough, the faint cry of "help" was heard floating on the soft night breeze.

"It sounds likes it's coming from that shopping center across the street," Officer Reed said. "I'll drive over and check it out."

The shopping center was L-shaped, and at the far right corner of the L was a drugstore. The officer turned the corner and stopped to listen. There it was again, and it was coming from the rooftop of the drugstore.

Climbing the old iron ladder bolted to the side of the

building, Officer Reed swept his flashlight slowly across the roof.

"Help me," cried a somewhat pitiful voice. "Over here . . . help!"

Reed's flashlight threw its light onto one of the building's ventilator shafts. Half a nose, two eyes, and the top of a man's head were all that were visible above the top of the vent. Like a deer frozen in the headlights, the helpless man stared blindly from the darkness. Officer Reed burst out laughing so hard it took him several attempts before he could yell those famous words: "*Freeze. Police!*" Then he burst into laughter again.

The shafted man didn't find the situation quite so funny, and let the officer know. Reed then called in and requested a rescue team to the scene.

Sometimes laughter can be infectious. This was one of those times. A cop's job is a dangerous and high-stress occupation that welcomes a little levity. Backup units began arriving. And laughing. The fire department arrived, along with an ambulance. They tried their best not to, but they laughed, too. Eventually, even the suspect began to laugh.

After several attempts to lift the man out, a power saw was used to cut a hole in the roof and remove the man and the vent all at once. The man was then cut out of the pipe and placed under arrest.

A routine frisk of the subject was cause for another outburst of laughter. The reason the man entered through the small vent, yet couldn't escape the same way, was that all of his pockets and the front of his shirt were stuffed with prescription drugs. The grateful goofball went on to tell Officer Reed that he was so excited to find all those drugs, he just didn't want to leave any behind.

The judge prescribed two years and to call him in the morning.

Perception Versus Reality

For some teenagers, committing dumb crimes is an occupational hazard that goes with the hormones. But two teenagers in Mesa, Arizona, deserve some sort of special recognition for their moronic accomplishment.

These two bozos shared a teenage paranoia—they were constantly checking their rear-view mirror for the lights of a police cruiser. This fear of cops gave them a brilliant idea for what they thought was a great gag. They stopped by an auto parts store and purchased some emergency lights for the roof of their car that were almost exactly like the ones on a police patrol car. Dumb and Dumber told the clerk they were volunteer firemen and needed the lights to answer calls.

With their blinding new emergency lights, the two teens began to freak out their friends with bogus "pullovers." In a rear-view mirror in the dark of night, they looked like the real deal to their friends—until they got right up to the driver's window and had a good laugh on their terrorized buds.

One night they were following a truck that looked just like one of their friend's pickups. The two pretend cops hit their lights and within moments the pickup had dutifully pulled over to the shoulder of the highway. But as Starsky and Crutch approached their "perp," they were stunned to see that the driver was not their friend, but a uniformed police officer who had just gotten off duty.

Dumber and Dumbest ran back to their "emergency" vehicle to beat a quick retreat, but the officer was too fast for them. They were quickly apprehended and arrested. Impersonating an officer is a serious offense, especially when the sucker you're trying to fool is no fool, but a uniformed cop.

No Olympic Gold for This Guy

Erica Peace's father was a deputy sheriff in Taney County, Missouri, and she remembers a few of the more interesting stories her late father told her. Today, Taney County is a busy place, because Branson has hit it big as an entertainment and vacation center. Back when Erica's father patrolled the country lanes, Branson was a quiet, quaint place where everybody knew everybody else. Even the county jail had several regulars, not unlike Andy Griffith's "Otis" in Mayberry.

One night two deputies were chasing one of these "regulars" for public drunkenness and fighting. Well, this "Otis" had a real brainstorm, or so he thought until he tried to pull off his escape. Otis was barely ahead of the two deputies who were chasing him on foot, when he leaped into the Lake of the Ozarks. See, he figured he could swim to the other side, step out of the water, and be free in Arkansas. Over there, the Missouri county officers couldn't touch him.

The would-be Mark Spitz got about fifty feet offshore when he began to tread water. The two deputies didn't really feel like getting wet, and they knew it was about half a mile across the lake, so they just stood on the shoreline tossing pebbles at the offender. After about ten minutes, the tired and waterlogged dummy gave up and swam back to shore, where the two deputies arrested him and escorted him to a nice dry cell.

How well do you know the dumb criminal mind?

What percentage of all vehicles stolen in the United States in 1995 were cars?

A. 61.
B. 43.
C. 78.

The correct answer is C. The America's Dumbest Criminals company car was stolen once and the thief captured. The case was thrown out by the judge, though. We could prove it was stolen . . . we just couldn't prove it was a car!

Safe . . . at First

"Go west, young man, go west!" Horace Greeley wrote those spirited words of wisdom a hundred years ago, and people have been headin' west ever since—drawn to the land of milk and honey with the cry of "There's gold in them there hills!" still ringing in their ears. Most are honest. Some are not.

In Corvallis, Oregon, the two men entering the large, two-story brick building from the roof that night were not honest. On the contrary. Their cry was, "There's gold in that thar safe!" This wasn't some spur-of-the-moment caper. While in prison, one of the men became friends with an inmate who used to work in this particular building. Both now knew the floor plan, when security made its rounds, and, most importantly, that there was a large safe inside. A payroll safe—and tomorrow was payday!

After climbing down a rope ladder to the second floor, they proceeded to the first floor and found the safe. It was huge. Break-in proof. But they had an equalizer. Why spend four hours hammering and drilling trying to knock off the tumbler when a few sticks of dynamite would do the job in seconds?

Why, indeed. Thirty seconds after lighting the fuses, they had their answer. In a tremendous explosion that practically leveled the building, the two were buried in a salvo of brick, wood, dirt, and debris. And that's where the police found them. After a stint in the hospital, both men were tried, convicted, and sentenced to prison.

What our two "dumbolition" experts didn't know was that the company that used to occupy the building had relocated. The old safe was too costly to move, so they sold it to the incoming construction company, which found it perfect for storage of their dynamite!

Con Descending

Known for its heavy winters, it's not uncommon in Fargo, North Dakota, to see someone up on a roof shoveling off the deep snow. And that's what this guy might have been doing, except for two things: He didn't have a shovel, and he was wearing only gloves and socks—in sub-zero weather.

Earl Buddly figured if he were going to break into the small five and dime, he would go in through the roof. Watching from the coffee shop across the street, he saw the employees file out at closing time. Twenty minutes later the owner locked up, got into his car, and drove away. Show time. Scaling a drain pipe in the rear corner of the building, our cautious criminal crawled to the skylight. He went to work with a crowbar, prying up a corner. With a little grunting and a big pop, the Plexiglas dome was removed.

Earl began to squirm and wiggle his way down. Hmmm . . . the opening was smaller than he had thought.

The opening was smaller than he had thought.

Aha! Too many clothes. Boots off, he undid his pants and quickly pulled them down to his ankles. That done, he dropped his boots and pants down to the floor below. He'd be going out the back door when he left.

Naked from the waist down except for his socks, he tried his descent once more. His bottom half fit, but now his top half was too big. So he climbed back out, whipped off the sweater and shirt, and tossed them down, too.

Now with both arms scissored above his head, he tried to squeeze his shoulders through the open skylight. No go. Covered with cuts and scrapes and nearly freezing, he gave up. His shoes and pants were lying fifteen feet below him in a nice warm pile on the floor. He began running in place and flapping his arms to keep warm. He was still flapping when the police arrived.

Thumbthing's Wrong

Back in Peoria, Illinois, some band members, buddies of mine, were setting up in a small club. The PA system was being tested while the drummer twisted the last wing-nut onto his cymbal stand. About then, the guitar player hurried in wheeling a large amplifier in front of him.

"Need some help?" the bass player called out from the stage.

"Nah, I got it. I just gotta get my 'ax' out of the back seat."

Moments later, the casual calm was shattered by a blood-curdling scream coming from the parking lot. "What the heck was that?" everyone asked in unison. Another scream cut through the air. The group scrambled from the stage and rushed outside. A man standing next to the guitar player's car was frantically pulling on the door handle with one hand and screaming bloody murder, dancing in place.

"Hey!" someone shouted, *"what the hell are you doin'?"*

More screams. The guitar case was lying on the ground at his feet. "Help me, please!" he begged. "Open the door for God's sake!"

My friend walked over and picked up his guitar. He looked at the man writhing in agony. "Damn, I'll bet that hurts," he said slowly.

"I think I'm gonna' faint!" cried the thief, "but I can't!" No he couldn't—not unless he wanted to lose an appendage.

While my friend was taking his amplifier inside the club, he was being watched. He had no more than gotten inside the building when the thief made his move. He opened the back door and, with his left hand on the roof, leaned inside and grabbed the guitar out of the backseat with his right hand. The thief swung the door shut. On his left thumb. And the door locked. It wasn't unlocked until the police arrived and arrested the guy.

Thumb fools never learn.

Herbal
Insulation

Working with juvenile offenders has got to be one of the most difficult jobs around, but it can also be the most rewarding. David Stevens of Middleville, Michigan, found out it can also be amusing.

David was a house parent at a juvenile detention facility and was always having serious discussions with his young charges. One day a youngster in the facility was telling David about his flannel-lined blue jeans. David had never heard of jeans that were insulated and told the young man he didn't believe him. "There's no such thing. I've never seen blue jeans with flannel lining."

The youngster was very indignant. "I've got some on. Look." To prove his point, the youngster loosened his belt and unzipped his fly to show David the flannel lining in his jeans. David saw the lining and had to admit that he was wrong, but he also saw the ounce of marijuana the kid had stuck in his pants. The kid had to laugh along with David at what an incredibly dumb thing he had just done. They both agreed the kid's jeans had too much lining to be legal.

The Dirty Dozen

As the officer was walking out of the Mesa, Arizona, police station, toward his squad car, he was struck by a flying doughnut. Thinking it was another officer just having some fun, he continued toward the lot. Two steps later he was pelted by another doughnut and still another. The last two strikes were thrown with force and, as far as the officer was concerned, the fun was over.

As the officer turned to locate the source of the barrage, another doughnut landed at his feet. Then he spotted a man standing in the shadows holding a small box. "What's your problem?" the officer wanted to know. "Is it the cops or the doughnuts you don't like?"

"Both," the man said dryly, reaching for another missile. Before you could say "dunk a doughnut," the man was arrested, handcuffed, and led into the station.

Inside the booking room, the sergeant took one look at the doughnutmeister and said, "Weren't you released from here not twenty minutes ago?"

"What's your problem?" the officer wanted to know. "Is it the cops
or the doughnuts you don't like?"

56

"Yeah, so what?" he said.

"So, what are you doin' back in here already?"

"Assault with a weapon on a police officer," the cop interjected.

"What kind of weapon?"

"Doughnuts!" the cop and Idiot said together.

The Sergeant peered into the box and then at the man. "They both look glazed to me," he said. "Okay, let's find a box for this guy." A box, that is, with three walls and a row of bars.

As best the officers could figure, after his release from jail some twenty minutes earlier, the man walked across the street to the doughnut shop, purchased a dozen glazed, walked back across the street, and began throwing them at the first cop he saw. The man was clearly a real (dough) nut case.

About Face

Here's a guy who really isn't a dumb criminal but could be considered criminally dumb.

Jeffrey Miles of North Wilkesboro, North Carolina, turned the key to his front door and entered the foyer. The house was dark except for the small kitchen light shining down the hallway. As he turned after closing the door, Miles saw a strange man—apparently an intruder— facing him in the dim light. With a loud yell, the home-owner bolted from his house, ran to neighbors, and phoned 911.

The officer who arrived was met at the curb by Miles and the neighbor. "He's still in there, I think. I haven't seen anyone leave since I called you. Be careful, officer," Miles advised.

"Did you get a good look at him?" the officer asked.

"I wasn't in there long enough for a good look, but I can tell you this, he was one ugly SOB!"

The cop crept up the front steps and entered the house

cautiously with weapon drawn. Miles and the neighbor waited outside at a safe distance. Thirty seconds later, the officer emerged from the house laughing uncontrollably.

"What is it?" Miles asked anxiously. "What'd you see in there?"

"C'mon up here, I want to show you something," the officer said, wiping tears of laughter from his eyes.

As the three men entered the house, the officer shined his light down the hallway. "There's your burglar, sir," the officer said.

"Well, I'll be damned," Miles said. The officer was still laughing. Miles and the neighbor joined in.

"I feel like a complete idiot," the homeowner said. "My wife told me she was going to do something with that full-length mirror she bought at the yard sale, but I didn't know she was going to put it at the end of the hallway! I guess I was wrong about an intruder in the house. . . . I'm sorry, officer."

"Well, you were right about one thing, though," the neighbor chimed in. "He was one ugly SOB!"

Knife Girls Finish Last

After pumping ten dollars' worth of gas, Susan Shriver of Mattoon, Wisconsin, pulled her car up by the front door of the all-night gas station and market. Once inside, she went over to the cooler and picked up two cases of cold beer. She hefted them onto the counter.

"That'll be twenty-eight dollars and eight cents," the clerk informed her.

The woman dug around in her purse for a moment, then told him that she'd left her money in the car. The clerk watched as she rummaged around in her front seat. A few seconds later she emerged with a ski mask on her head (not over her face, *on her head*) and re-entered the store. She pulled the ski mask down over her face and whipped out a knife.

"I'm takin' this beer!" she exclaimed, "and don't try to stop me or I'll cut you up!"

The clerk, realizing that the women's straw didn't go

"I'm takin' this beer!" she exclaimed, "and don't try to stop me or I'll cut you up!"

all the way to the bottom of her glass, asked, "Are you gonna pay for the gas?"

She was stunned. "Say what? I'm stealin' the beer. Why would I pay for the gas?"

While Shriver was carrying the beer out to the car, the clerk hit the hot line button under the counter that dials 911. When the woman came back for the second case of beer, she noticed a collection jar on the counter. She lifted up her ski mask and peered inside. Without hesitation she grabbed the jar, set it on top of the second case of beer, got into her car, and pulled away. A pretty good haul—darned near forty dollars worth of stuff!

Well, she barely made it out of the parking lot before she was surrounded by the local cops. She was arrested and charged with felony armed robbery. Forty dollars might not seem like much, but when you spread it out over five years, it's even less.

The Telltale Hat

Will Rogers once said, "God picked up the United States and shook it, and everything that was loose fell into California." He wasn't kidding, as in the case of the Oakland, California, robber who victimized an elderly woman.

The thief came out of nowhere. "Give me all your money!" he demanded.

Fearing for her safety, the victim complied, giving up her pocketbook and some rings. Running hard, but still in full view of the victim, the thief felt his hat blow off his head, and it (the hat, not his head) landed in the middle of the sidewalk. The police were called, and the hat was picked up and marked as evidence.

A few days later the elderly victim was asked if she would come down to the station that afternoon to view a police lineup of potential suspects. She agreed, but it all happened so fast and scared her so, she really didn't get that good a look at the man. But she would try.

At the police station, she was taken to a small room and seated behind a two-way mirror. Seven men stood lined up on the other side of the glass. One by one, the men were ordered to place the mugger's hat on their heads, step forward and say, "Give me all your money!" After the last man had spoken, the detective turned to the lady and said, "Well, do you recognize one of them as the robber?"

She shook her head slowly back and forth while biting her lower lip. "I . . . I can't be certain. . . . I'm sorry, young man, I'm just not sure."

"I understand," he said gently. He then picked up the microphone. "All right, fellas, that'll be all, thank you."

The victim rose up from her chair, still shaking her head. Suddenly, the man in the middle of the lineup yelled to the officer just offstage, "Hey, can I have my hat back?"

Now, we're curious: Just what size hat fits a pinhead?

The Perfect Witness

After picking up a few items at a convenience store in Birmingham, Alabama, a middle-aged man was halfway out the door, when a young man in his twenties barged past him, looking a little nervous and certainly in a big hurry.

From his vantage point directly in front of the store window, the man watched as the kid suddenly pulled a knife on the cashier. The clerk reached into the cash drawer and handed the robber a fistful of bills. Stuffing the money into his pants, the kid raced from the store and into a pickup truck parked right beside the stunned man. Tires squealing, the truck sped away. The man was shaken. He had just witnessed an armed robbery.

Within moments of the clerk's shaky 911 call, the police arrived in force. The witness related to the officers exactly what he had seen and was able to describe the robber and the getaway truck in vivid detail. Police thanked him and he went straight home.

About ten miles from the robbery, the pickup was found abandoned on the side of the road, where it had apparently broken down. At about the same time the police were going over the truck, the eyewitness received a phone call from his son. It seems his truck had broken down on the side of the road and he needed someone to pick him up.

Well, needless to say, someone did. And it wasn't Dad. After a heated conversation, the son was persuaded to surrender to the authorities. Which he did.

The young son couldn't offer his father one good reason for robbing the store. But had the young man taken just a moment to look around, a good reason for not robbing the store would have been, shall we say, "apparent."

A Lot of Dollars . . . But No Sense

This story out of Houston, Texas, confirms what cops have been tellin' us for years: "There's no such thing as a routine traffic stop."

While officer Joe Aldaco was running radar on a busy Houston street, a black Cadillac streaked by at seventy miles an hour. Officer Aldaco gave chase and quickly pulled the vehicle over to the side of the road.

"The reason I stopped you," he informed the woman driving the car, "is that the speed limit along this road is fifty-five. I clocked you at seventy miles an hour."

"Yeah, well, I'm in a hurry," she snapped back.

Inside the car, the officer saw a disheveled pile of hundreds, fifties, and twenties scattered across the front seat. "Where did you get that money?" he asked.

"That's my money!" she blurted. "Just give me the ticket, will ya?"

Then, Officer Aldaco spotted a bank bag next to the money. "Ma'am," he repeated his original question, "where did you get all that money?"

"I told you, jerk, that's my money!"

"I need to see your driver's license and proof of insurance," he told her.

"My license has been suspended, and I don't have any insurance," she replied.

With that, the officer asked her to step out of the vehicle and informed her that she was being arrested for driving on a suspended license, no insurance, and speeding. Officer Aldaco confiscated the money and the bank bag from the front seat of her car. Again he asked the woman where she got the money.

She'd had enough. "I just robbed a bank, okay? And it's my money!"

Dispatch confirmed that a local bank had indeed been robbed not thirty minutes earlier by a woman who drove off in a black Cadillac.

The lesson to be learned? If you steal money, drive crazy, don't have a valid driver's license, and insult the police, you're going to jail. And that you can bank on!

DUMB CRIMINAL QUIZ NO. 911

How well do you know the dumb criminal mind?

With the aid of a store security camera, police in Lancaster, Pennsylvania, were able to identify and catch the armed robber of a convenience store. Was it because . . .

- A. The man was a former employee?
- B. He had just been released from prison for the same crime? or
- C. He wore a basketball jersey with a team name on the front, and his last name on the back.

You guessed it. The correct answer is C. What a good sport!

Two-Way Radio ... One-Way Ticket

Responding to a silent alarm at an industrial park in Aurora, Colorado, police officer Dave Leonard arrived at the location along with two other units. It wasn't long before he noticed a large garage door with a panel broken out of it.

Officer Leonard went around to the side of the garage and looked in a window. Not two feet away from him he saw a man with a black stocking cap atop his head, stacking up boxes by the side door.

"Hey, you supposed to be in there?" Officer Leonard asked calmly.

"No," the man replied matter-of-factly.

"I want you to come out here and talk to me."

The man did as he was instructed, exiting the garage by the side door.

"What are you doing in there?" he was asked.

"Nothin'," he stated. After a brief interview, the subject was placed under arrest for burglary.

As the fool was being read his rights, a whispered voice came over a radio. "Unit One to Unit Two. Unit One to Unit Two. Come in, Unit Two." But the source wasn't a police radio. It was coming from a walkie-talkie set the suspect was wearing on his belt.

"Who's that?" the officer asked.

"That's my partner," the guy admitted. "He's driving around while I steal stuff. I'm supposed to let him know when I'm ready for him to come back and pick me up."

Without looking at the suspect, Officer Leonard played a hunch. "Tell him that you're ready for him to pick you up."

"Okay," the man complied. "Unit Two to Unit One. Come in, Unit One."

"One here," came the reply.

"Come and get me. Over."

"On my way."

He was on his way all right—to jail. Unit Two was arrested as he pulled up. The car was impounded and both U—nitwits were taken into custody.

 **Rocket Man**

When one intentionally breaks the law and gets caught, he automatically becomes a dumb criminal. Even the smart ones.

Palmer Destry was brilliant. He worked at a jet propulsion lab in Pasadena, California. His was a high-paying job that earned him respect among his peers and a hefty salary to boot. But when five o'clock rolled around, Destry would begin his second job in another laboratory—in the basement of his exclusive high-dollar suburban home. Here, he wasn't formulating advanced rocket science. He was manufacturing the highly addictive and very illegal methamphetamine, otherwise known as crystal meth.

Destry took pride in his work. With his background in chemical engineering, he was convinced that his product was the finest money could buy. He was so enamored with his talent and the product he produced, he documented his genius. With a super-8 video camera

As writer, director, and star of the show, our egghead took us through his illegal lab step-by-step.

mounted on a tripod, he created his own "infomercial." As writer, director, and star of the show, our egghead took us through his illegal lab step-by-step. He was ever so thorough in describing it.

Just as it is with all good things, all bad things must come to an end. Acting on a tip from a credible police informant, narcotics agents were able to obtain a search warrant, which they served early one morning on the unsuspecting Mr. Smug. Along with a mountain of evidence seized at his home, the video infomercial was confiscated as well.

At the trial, Destry's home movie proved to be the fatal nail in the proverbial coffin for our Captain Vidiot. He was found guilty on all charges and sent to prison for a long, long, time.

As one of the testifying officers put it, "This was one case where the drug dealer really was a rocket scientist!"

The Revolving Door of Justice

The Tarrant County Sheriff's Department in Fort Worth, Texas, is still laughing.

A known car thief had just been arrested for the umpteenth time. Having been through this drill before, he posted bond within two hours and walked out the front door, a free man. The jailers were stunned when police brought the same character in through the back door seventeen minutes later.

The Fort Worth officer told them this idiot had gone to the parking lot adjacent to the jail and was caught trying to steal another car. The professional bungler's excuse— he didn't have money for a cab. When crime statistics say a car is stolen every seventeen minutes, they don't mean by the same thief . . . or do they?

Scratching the Surface

Police Chief Allen L. Muma of Mantum, Michigan, gave us this story of a juvenile "DUHlinquent" who was dumb enough to commit the crime and then stupid enough to solve it.

During a shift change at the police station one evening, a patrol officer noticed that some unknown had carved numerous obscenities on the cage in his squad car that separates the prisoners from the police. According to Chief Muma, it had been an especially busy day and the culprit could have been any of a dozen people the officer had transported. Chalking it up as "it comes with the job," they decided to let it go.

Months passed and the incident had long since been forgotten, when, while patrolling his sector, the officer whose car had been vandalized was approached by a half dozen juveniles. One of the youths, a known trouble-maker who'd been arrested on numerous occasions, asked the officer if he could show his buddies the back seat of the squad car. Happy to oblige, the officer opened the back door and was stunned when the kid pointed to the obscene graffiti scratched into the cage and began bragging to the others that this was some of his handiwork.

He was arrested on the spot and charged with malicious destruction of police property.

"So it is written . . . so it shall be dumb."

Some Moxie Morons

Once wasn't enough, so a few Mantua, Ohio, teenagers figured they would vent their adolescent angst and hormonal overflow by vandalizing their school system's buses—a second time. In the darkness, they scaled the fence alongside the County School System parking lot. With no one around, the morons began spray painting and slashing.

The punks were working on the third bus when a deputy happened to spot the kids in action. He called for backup and, within moments, four officers had chased the radial radicals down. Asked why they had done it, the youngsters shrugged their shoulders and explained, "Well, you didn't catch us the last time."

Aha! That explains the unsolved vandalism to the buses just a month earlier. Two cases closed.

The Safe That Held Up Two Robbers

In Lake Oswego, Oregon, a couple of bad guys found out the hard way that "two out of three" ain't bad . . . but it ain't good enough.

The plan to steal the safe was sound; the two men in the parking lot agreed to that. They would back up the big truck to the front of the store, run in, and wrap the thick chain around the floor safe and pull it right out of the store. Unless something unforeseen happened, they figured their chances of a clean getaway were pretty good.

They'd done their homework. They were familiar with the store, knew on what day the safe was full, and had tracked how often the police made their rounds. Both men were keenly aware that their success depended on three things—expedient execution, split-second timing, and a little luck.

Their execution was flawless. By screaming "Everybody down!" as they entered the store, they got what they were counting on—confusion, fear, and compliance.

Their timing was impeccable. In less than thirty seconds the heavy chain had been wrapped twice around the safe and held fast by the large hook placed over the taut links.

Their luck, however, was terrible. With his adrenaline pumping, the driver mashed the pedal to the metal and he didn't let up. The force of the initial thrust jerked the safe off the floor and sent it sliding out the front door at about twenty miles an hour. When the safe had cleared the entrance way, the driver slammed on the brakes. The truck stopped. The safe didn't.

To the amazement of our two Robin Hoodlums, that big ol' safe just kept a' comin'. Out the door, across a short sidewalk, into the parking lot, and straight for the rear end of their pickup.

"Go, man, go!" the guy ridin' shotgun screamed.

"I'm goin', I'm goin'!" snapped his partner. The driver hit the gas at the exact same moment the safe hit them. With the grating screech of metal on metal, coupled with a bone-jarring crash, the rear end of the truck was lifted off the ground as the safe wedged itself beneath the frame.

The smell of burning rubber filled the air as blue smoke rolled from the squealing back tires. The speedometer said ninety; the thieves said nothing. As for the plan, five points for loyalty, five years for stupidity.

The Mental ...Patient Bank Robber

Fort Lauderdale, Florida—home of fabulous beaches, pretty women, and dumb criminals.

The man stood calmly in line at the bank awaiting his turn. "Next!" a soft voice called. The man walked up to the counter and handed a sheet of paper to the teller. It was a holdup note demanding that a large sum of money be placed into a bank bag and handed over to him.

The quick-thinking teller told the man that she didn't have that much in her drawer and it might take a few minutes to get it together. The man said okay, and casually walked back to the end of the line. Seizing the opportunity, the teller phoned an employee upstairs and filled her in on what was happening. That employee could see the man in line through her office window. She called 911.

She was still on the phone with the dispatcher as police arrived and surrounded the bank. By the time the area was cleared and the SWAT team arrived, a full fifteen minutes had elapsed. The man approached the teller.

"Ready yet?" he asked.

"Almost," she replied. Just then her phone rang. It was the girl upstairs.

"The police said to go ahead and give him the money," she whispered. The teller complied.

With bank bag in hand, the man exited the building and was immediately set upon by the police. By now, twenty minutes had gone by since he had handed the teller his stickup note.

Pretty dumb, huh? Dig this. The holdup note the suspect had mindlessly left behind was written on the back of a job application he had filled out. His name, address, phone number, blood type, shoe size, and religious affiliation were right there in black and white—the same color as the car that gave him a free lift to jail.

How well do you know the dumb criminal mind?

In Indianapolis, Indiana, Bobby Swope broke into his neighbor's house and stole a gun. Was he caught because . . .

A. He was arrested for DUI and the weapon found under the seat was traced to the rightful owner?

B. The gun didn't work, so he broke back into the house to return it? or

C. The phony gun dealer he tried to sell it to was an undercover cop?

The correct answer is B. B-lieve it or not, when Swope discovered that the weapon didn't work, he broke back into the house to return it. That's when he was caught by the police!

Where There's a Will, There's a Spray

This story of woe begins and ends in Harvey, Louisiana. A teenage girl approached a man loading his van with boxes for delivery. As he started to get into the van, the young girl walked up to him and demanded the keys to the van. The man refused. The juvenile whipped out a knife.

"Now gimme the keys!" she demanded. The driver tossed her the keys. The youngster hopped in, started the van, and sat there for several minutes. Apparently unable to drive a stick shift, the frustrated teen exited the van and ran off. The driver called the cops.

A few blocks from the scene of her original attempt, she again tries to hijack a vehicle. This time it's an exterminator's truck. She swiped at the man with her knife and grabbed for the keys. The man jumped back, and with the wand attached to a canister of bug spray, fought off her first attempt to cut him.

She was relentless. Again and again she attempted to

The man opted for chemical warfare. . . . *"Take that!"* he cried.

get to him with her knife, and each time her thrusts were parried by the exterminator. Fencing for his life, the man opted for chemical warfare. He began pumping up the pressure on his tank with his left hand. "*Take that!*" he cried, unleashing a pressurized stream of pesticide into the deranged girl's face. Coughing and sputtering and half-blinded by the spray, the girl gave up and ran off. Now he called the cops.

Needless to say, the police were on the lookout for a young girl carrying a knife and reeking of bug spray. Moments later a patrol officer spotted the girl. He gave her chase on foot and was about to apprehend her when she suddenly turned and tried to slash him. More chemical warfare. Coughing and gagging again, this time from pepper spray, the girl was subdued and arrested.

The disturbed girl was booked on two counts of attempted carjacking, five counts of assault, and one count of resisting arrest by flight. *Whew!*

Drop in Any Time

A cat burglar entered a grocery store in Vermilion, Ohio, from the roof one night. Lacking the stealth and balance of a real feline, our creature of the night ended up falling through the ceiling and into the middle of a crew busy restocking the shelves for the next day's customers. Our falling star was quickly set upon by the startled crew and arrested by the local police.

Oh yeah, the store was an all-night market—it stayed open twenty-four hours. So did the front door!

34 A Field of Bad Dreams

The journey of C. J. Courtly begins in Denver, takes us to Indianapolis, and ends up in Oberlin, Kansas.

The trip was going well, and why shouldn't it? Besides having ten bricks of marijuana concealed in the trunk of his car, Cunning Courtly had broken no laws. He didn't speed, he used his turn signal, and he never tailgated. Police had virtually no cause to pull him over.

But C. J. pulled over for his own reasons. It was nearly midnight, and the three cups of coffee that he'd downed at a truck stop were now demanding a pit stop. He was careful to lock all the doors after he got out of the car. He stuck his keys in his back pocket and walked a ways into the pitch-black field beside the highway to do his business.

While relieving himself, he realized that a second nature call was unavoidable, but he was too close to the road. So he walked a good distance farther, dropped his drawers, completed his business, and walked back to the car. He reached for the keys in his back pocket but they weren't there. Panicked, he quickly searched his remaining pockets. No keys. They must've fallen out of his pocket when he lowered his pants.

Retracing his footsteps in total darkness, a half-hour search turned up nothing. He was stranded. He peered through the darkness across the wheat field. A light. A farmhouse. Maybe he could get some help there.

After a good half mile, he finally reached the farmhouse. Dogs began to bark. Soon a porch light came on and a young man appeared at the door. Not quite sure how to explain his predicament, the smuggler stepped back into the shadows by a clump of trees and nervously chewed on his thumbnail.

Unbeknownst to our troubled traveler, the farmhouse belonged to the local sheriff. He wasn't home at the time but his son was. Alerted by the barking dogs, he'd looked out the window and seen the man's retreat into the woods. He phoned the sheriff's office and reported a stranger on the property. Fifteen minutes later the deputy sheriff pulled into the front yard.

"How ya' doin', officer?" he said.

"Just fine, sir. Do you live around here?"

"No," he responded, "I live in Indianapolis."

"What's your name?" the officer pressed.

"I'm C. J. Courtly."

"Oh, then that must be your car back there on the highway," added the deputy, who had already run the tag number.

"Car? No, I don't know what you're talking about. I don't have a car on the highway."

After a series of common-sense questions that elicited only nonsense answers, the deputy arrested C. J. A search warrant was issued and the car impounded. The bricks of marijuana were discovered, and our leading candidate for President of the Liar's Club was charged with interstate transportation of marijuana with intent to sell.

With a choice between following the law of nature and the law of man, this guy obeyed the wrong one.

Trés Amigos Stupidos

Two secretaries returning from lunch in Oklahoma City, Oklahoma, spotted three men riffling through cars parked along the street next to their office building. When the suspects saw the women approaching, they began walking away. As the men passed by the secretaries, one of the women asked them what they were doing.

"We're lost," one replied nervously in broken English.

"Where is it that you're trying to get to?" asked the woman.

"3524 South Adams Street," came the reply.

Familiar with the downtown area, the secretary directed them to the general area.

"Something about them isn't right," stated one worker as they got upstairs.

"Hey, everybody," spoke the other, "there were three guys down there messing with some cars on the street. If

91

your car is parked on the street, you might want to see if anything's missing."

Heeding their advice, several employees went downstairs to take a look.

A few minutes later one of the car owners returned upstairs. "They got my mobile phone," he said dejectedly. The police were called. The secretaries told them what had happened and told them the address the men said they were looking for.

Twenty minutes later, the police returned and asked the ladies to ID the three men in the back of the squad car. As the two women were positively identifying the three men, the phone on the waistband of one of them began to ring. The man tried to answer it, but he wasn't quite sure how. One of the policemen answered it for him—it was the employee upstairs watching from the window.

Between the two eyewitnesses and the phone call, the men were promptly arrested. So, how was it that the police were able to find these men so easily? Simple. The three didn't speak much English, but they did know the address of the construction site where they were working. It was 3524 South Adams Street. Come to find out they were illegal aliens and were immediately deported.

Adios, Hombres!

Dudley Do-Wrong

Ken Simpson is a correctional officer in the Canadian province of British Columbia, and he sent us a detailed report of a not-so-Great Escape by one less-than-lucky inmate.

This particular prisoner was actually fairly well-behaved. In fact, he was what Ken would call a model inmate. He was allowed to go outside the prison on daily work details, which are breaths of fresh air to a prisoner who has been cooped up in a workhouse.

One day on work detail, one of our gent's fellow inmates fell ill. While the guards were busy attending to the puny prisoner, Mr. Model Behavior seized the moment and was able to slip off and make a run for it. Within five minutes the escapee had broken into a car and hot-wired the ignition. He headed down the freeway toward what seemed to be a flawless escape.

There were only two problems:

Number One: The stolen car had virtually no gas in it.

93

Number Two: The freeway entrance he had chosen was on a steep hill, with the Royal Canadian Mounted Police Station right there.

As soon as our Steve McQueen started up the steep hill onto the freeway, his getaway car stuttered, lurched, and coughed its way to a stop, out of gas—directly in front of the police station. As he frantically tried to restart the stolen car, two officers came out of the station and noticed the nervous guy with car trouble. Always ready to help a citizen in distress, the two officers approached the man to render what assistance they could. Of course, the motorist insisted he was fine.

Unfortunately for Stevo, one of the officers had already noticed the car had been hot-wired. It was at that moment the report of the escape came across the other officer's radio. The three of them all listened to a perfect description of the motorist in distress.

The prisoner just put out his hands to be cuffed.

More Than a Swap on the Wrist

A small town in Mississippi was honored to be home to the county's high school. This meant that the tiny burg of fifteen hundred citizens actually grew twice its normal size during school hours. And like any growing metropolis, the town began to have crime problems.

One night the high school was broken into by thieves who entered through a kitchen fan. The sheriff and his deputies arrived just after the thieves departed the building through the front door, tripping the alarm. There were very few clues and no suspects. It was about six the next morning when the local radio station went on the air with news of the daring high school heist, which was followed by the station's most popular show, *The Swap Meet.* The on-air personality would take calls from people who wanted to trade items for what was offered over the air.

The sheriff and his deputies were doing paperwork on the crime when the disc jockey started the swapping.

"All right, our first item, or should I say items, are ten space heaters that Bobby Monet has to trade for a late-model Corvette or Trans Am. Bobby also has four trombones that he would like to trade for a VCR."

One deputy was writing the words "space heaters" on the list of missing items when he heard Bobby Monet put the missing items up for trade on *The Swap Meet*. One of the deputies owned a 1969 Trans Am, and within two hours the deputy, dressed in plain clothes, met Bobby to show him his vintage Trans Am. Within moments four deputies had apprehended Bobby Monet and swapped him five years in jail for the space heaters and trombones.

We Haven't Been Properly Introduced

Late one night in a small town in the state of Washington, a woman heard a noise coming from a back bedroom. Her husband had run to the grocery, so she went into the hallway and said, "Bob, is that you?"

A young man stuck his head out of the bedroom door and said, "No, I'm Brian."

She screamed and ran to the phone to call the cops. Brian took off. Moments later the police responded, but as they approached the woman's house, they passed a car with a young man driving. Knowing the suspect's description and his first name, they pulled the young man over and asked, "Are you Brian?"

"Yes, sir."

The wheels of justice turn so much faster when the criminals introduce themselves politely.

Thinking fast, she gave the mystery man a sales pitch on her cleaning services.

Honey, There's Someone at the Door

Dumb criminals are people like you and us. They put their pants on one leg at a time. They eat and sleep just like we do, and when the doorbell rings, they open the door, even when they're robbing someone's house.

A cleaning lady in Cambridge, Massachusetts, had arrived at her next appointment. She rang the doorbell before she used her key to get in. The man who answered was not the owner, and he was wearing white socks on his hands. Thinking fast, she gave the mystery man a sales pitch on her cleaning services.

"Not interested. Thanks."

With that, the burglar closed the door and finished his job. The cleaning lady alerted the police. Within moments the cops arrived at the house and caught Sad Sock as he was leaving with the loot.

40 A Reversal of Fortune

Troopers with the Alaska Highway Patrol observed a car with two occupants driving erratically. After a half mile or so, the troopers had seen enough. They popped on their lights, gave a blast on the siren, and the car pulled over.

As one of the troopers stepped from his vehicle, the driver awkwardly tried to change places with the passenger. While the two boozed-up buffoons struggled to crawl over each other, one of them hit the gear shift and sent the car into reverse. The other drunk tried to step on the brake, but hit the gas instead. They rammed the patrol car.

As it turns out, both car occupants tested positive for driving under the influence. They also tested positive for total stupidity.

Easy Reader

Early in his career, police officer John Jenkins was on the force of a small town in Ohio. He responded to a call one morning about a break-in at the clubhouse of a local motorcycle gang. Upon his arrival, Jenkins saw a window had been broken out. The burglar had apparently reached in through the broken glass, unlocked it, and climbed in. Several cases of beer were missing.

As Officer Jenkins looked around, he spotted a rolled-up magazine with about fifty rubber bands around it. There was broken glass on the frayed edges, and he deduced that this was what the thief had used to break the window. Unrolling the magazine, the officer chuckled as he read the mailing label, complete with name, address, and zip code. This house was a stone's throw away.

Looking out the broken window in the direction of the house, Jenkins saw an unopened beer can lying on the ground. Then another. He walked outside and began to follow them. The trail led him into a small wooded area.

Still clutching the magazine, he continued through the woods. A short distance later, the woods gave way to a clearing and more beer cans leading up to a house—with the same address as the one on the magazine. *Looks like the boys in forensics could take the night off,* Jenkins thought, chuckling to himself.

To make a short story a little longer, the man was arrested and charged with breaking and entering, theft, and possession of stolen property.

It clearly was a case of beer . . . and a major case of stupidity.

Of Mice and Ex-Boyfriends

Neil Sedaka said it best years ago in his rock 'n' roll ballad "Breaking Up Is Hard to Do." Some people make it as hard as they can, and who knows how better than your beloved? Your beloved knows your dreams and your insecurities, your pet peeves and your greatest fears.

Tom H. in Massachusetts had fallen out of love. He wanted to let Sally know that she was a great person, but for whatever reason, "they" were just not meant to be. Tom let her down gently. Sally, on the other hand, wanted to hurt Tom real bad, and she knew exactly how to do it, even if it meant taking the law—and some rodents—into her own hands.

Tom was six-foot-four and two hundred pounds, and he worked out. Sally was maybe a hundred and ten pounds and all of five-foot-three. What could this diminutive demon do to this hulking bully?

You see, Tom had confided his greatest fear to Sally a

Tom had confided his greatest fear to Sally a while back and, unfortunately for him, Sally remembered.

104

while back and, unfortunately for him, Sally remembered. She went to Tom's apartment and displayed two mice in a tiny cage. Then, with Tom shaking and screaming, she released the mice under the covers of Tom's bed and left.

Police answered Tom's call for help. When they got there, Tom was on top of his refrigerator squealing like a small child.

Touché, Sally.

Cousin Ninny

Every region of our country has its own set of stereotypes when it comes to how they regard residents on the other coast or even in the neighboring county. One of the reasons these stereotypes live on is, every now and then somebody comes through town who really does embody the worst characteristics of a strange and alien culture.

Everyone in the world can describe an obnoxiously direct and arrogant person who (allegedly) typifies the Big Apple. One officer in Virginia met an incredibly blunt New Yorker who talked himself right into jail.

The man had been clocked at eighty in a sixty-five zone. He had to appear before a judge and pay a fine if found guilty, and then he would be back on the road. The judge immediately noticed the young man's accent and asked him where he was from.

"New York, of course."

The judge nodded. "And you're here for a traffic violation, correct?"

"Yes . . . yes, your honor," the impatience in his voice creeping through.

"Well, what brings you to Virginia?" the judge asked, making cordial conversation while stamping the guy's file.

"I'm running some coke for a friend and I really need to get moving."

Everyone in the courtroom stopped for a moment in disbelief, and then burst into laughter. A subsequent search of Broadway Bozo's car proved his story beyond the shadow of a doubt. He was in jail in a New York minute.

Shopping in Altered States

Officer Michael Maloney of Langhorne, Pennsylvania, was at roll call when he was alerted to a problem down the street at the Mega High Discount Mall. The radio described a car being chased by the security truck out of the mall, toward the police station.

As Maloney hit the doors to the parking lot, he could already see the yellow flashing lights of the mall security truck coming slowly down the street behind a weaving Toyota. The woman at the wheel pulled into the police station parking lot and jerked her car in park. She approached Officer Maloney with something in her hand.

"Here." The obviously inebriated lady handed over a brand new camcorder she had just shoplifted. The security guy said he had followed her half a block, when she pulled over to ask him why he was following her. He explained; but she said, "If you don't stop following me, I'm going to call the cops."

"Fine. They're two doors down. Second drive on the left."

Maloney had been on duty only seven minutes, and he had already nabbed a fleeing criminal, retrieved stolen property, and booked a DUI. That's got to be some sort of record.

They're Sitting on Top of the Loot

Cracking ATMs is a crime ripe for dummies. It's what we call the "Impossible Dream."

A couple of fellas in Portland, Oregon, decided to take the ATM challenge one night. They had a powerful 4 x 4 and had a stout chain for towing cars, so they were ready for anything.

About two in the morning, they backed up to a free-standing ATM kiosk. One of the slick dudes wrapped the chain around the ATM and signaled the driver. That sports utility vehicle groaned in the lowest gear and then screeched off. The front wheels popped off the pavement when the slack snapped out of the chain. With a grinding rip, the ATM came free from its foundation.

Phase 1 was complete and they gave each other high-fives. Phase 2 now began. The plan was to tow the ATM until it cracked open. They towed the metal ATM five or six blocks, and every time it bounced into the air and came crashing back down on the pavement, it made a

110

The plan was to tow the ATM until it cracked open.

horrible racket. The farther they went, the more impenetrable the ATM seemed to be.

A brilliant solution came to them. They would release the ATM and smash into it with their 4 x 4. Surely, that would free up the cash inside. They took a running start half a block from it. They must have been doing fifty or sixty miles per hour when they hit. *Wham, bam,* and suddenly silence.

They were sitting three feet in the air with their wheels barely touching the road. Their 4 x 4 was suspended in the air, stuck on top of their loot, the ATM. They were still spinning their tires when the police arrived.

This is the only known case of an ATM solving its own burglary and physically holding the culprits at the scene until the police arrived.

"Ask a Simple Question . . ."

Several years ago, as a rookie deputy sheriff in New Mexico, Captain Billy Hillgartner was practicing lifting fingerprints with rubber fingerprint lifters. Having successfully lifted one of his own prints from his desk, he tossed this print into his briefcase and forgot it.

About a month later Hillgartner was interviewing a burglary suspect at his desk and getting nowhere. The guy was not admitting to anything, and Billy really had nothing on him. This guy was a pro and Hillgartner was just a rookie.

At wit's end, Billy just happened to glance over at his briefcase and he spotted the old fingerprint lifter. He pulled the lifter out and showed it to his suspect.

"Do you know what this is?" he asked, and tossed it across the desk to the suspect.

The suspect picked it up and, after looking at it, replied, "Yes."

Hillgartner then asked the suspect a simple question: "Do you know where I got that?"

The suspect lowered his head and again replied, "Yes, 4712 Donaldson Lane."

Hillgartner couldn't believe his ears. The guy then gave a full confession.

In fact, Hillgartner's ploy has worked with six guys. His own fingerprint helped him solve at least six different burglaries.

Enter and Sign In, Please

A young gentleman entered a motel lobby in Sacramento, California, and waited patiently as the night clerk finished registering another guest. As the clerk ran the first customer's credit card, she handed our young male visitor a registration card to fill out while waiting. As the first customer left the lobby for a good night's sleep, the clerk turned to the young gentleman and said, "May I help—"

The gun in our young man's hand stopped the clerk's heart cold. She was told to give him all the cash, which she did. The young gentleman fled the lobby. The entire crime took about as much time to commit as it took you to read about it. Within five minutes, the police arrived. They asked the clerk for a description of her assailant and details of the robbery. That's when she gave the cops the thief's registration card.

He had entered his *real* name, his *real* address, and his *real* car license tag number. The address he gave was only three blocks away, so the cops dropped in while they were in the neighborhood. There was our young gentleman lying on his bed, counting his cash. Next up— a free stay at the 365 Days Inn.

How to Collar a Crook from Your Recliner

You'd think that in Hawaii, lovebirds would coo blissfully all day. But as officer Ron Parker of Wailuku can tell you, there is sometimes trouble in paradise.

One night Officer Parker and his partner responded to a domestic violence call in their sector. As they drove to the residence, they passed a man dressed only in shorts and carrying a large duffel bag.

Moments later, the man's wife described him to the officers, right down to his shorts. Parker left his partner to take the woman's statement and then went to pick up the fleeing hubby. Five blocks away, Parker pulled over behind him, popped on his lights, and gave a little bleep from his siren.

The guy ran for it. Well, he began trotting at least. Parker patiently pursued the slow-jogging perpetrator by holding steady at seven miles an hour. After about two miles of fairly serious roadwork, the sweaty hubby collapsed under the weight of his duffel bag and crumpled

As they drove to the residence, they passed a man dressed only in shorts and carrying a large duffel bag.

118

to the pavement, huffing and puffing. Parker pulled alongside, rolled down the window and asked politely, "Would you like to get in the back?"

The man gathered his belongings and stepped into the squad car. Parker had just executed a chase and capture without even leaving his squad car. Book 'em, Dano!

DUMB CRIMINAL QUIZ NO. 714

How well do you know the dumb criminal mind?

After buying several high-dollar items with a stolen credit card, was the thief caught after he . . .

A. Tried to return some merchandise for cash?
B. Tried to purchase something from the store owner that owned the card?
C. Paid his water bill with the stolen credit card?

The correct answer is C. Water you thinkin'?

I'll Be Right Back

Bermuda is not a big place. If you're a local and you pull a job in Bermuda, the odds are someone will know it's you. Yet, a local still decided to take his shot at the perfect crime.

First, he scouted the bank. A tape from the surveillance camera clearly shows him eyeballing the security devices, walking around the bank in a very colorful, very conspicuous shirt with a number on it. The tape shows the same man, in the same shirt, re-enter the bank wearing a ski mask.

The victims, witnesses, and bystanders all had the same story.

"Joe just robbed the bank."

Two officers went to Joe's house and picked him up. Everything is slower and simpler on an island, even crime.

50 Lassie to the Rescue

Frank Wise of Cordele, Georgia, tells us the story of a patrolman who one night came across two young men acting strangely in a cemetery. After backup arrived, the officer began a search of their car for drugs, when, suddenly, one of the suspects bolted, dodging headstones. He leaped over a ditch and darted into a nearby residential neighborhood. It looked like his speed and luck would lose the police.

Within moments, however, the chase abruptly halted. When they caught up, the officers approached the man, flat on his back screaming for help. Over him was a vicious-looking dog, growling and snarling with one paw firmly planted on the fugitive's neck. The grounded suspect complained that the dog bit his leg and tripped him. Every time the suspect tried to get up, the dog would snap at his face and push him down with a paw to the throat. He begged the police to call off their K-9 officer, but they couldn't. It wasn't their dog.

Their K-9 officer was on sick leave. The dog that so deftly apprehended the fleeing felon was a stray. The owner of the house came out to see what all the fuss was about. When he heard how the dog had protected his property, the home owner adopted him, built him a dog-house, and fenced in his backyard. He figured any dog that protected him so well deserved a home for life. The criminal found a home as well, but only for five to seven years.

Wait, You Already Were a Winner

James Misson and his boss were closing down their electronics store for the night in Lakehurst, New Jersey, but they had to wait for one last customer to leave. The woman appeared to be browsing, but when she saw they were about to lock up, she hurried toward the exit. For some reason, she looked very familiar to Misson and his boss.

That's when the alarm sounded. The woman had lifted one nine-volt battery worth a couple bucks. The two store workers called the cops, who got to the scene quickly and issued the woman a ticket before turning her loose.

That's when it hit Misson. The woman had won a store contest the week before, the prize a camcorder worth over a thousand dollars. So much for gratitude.

Bigger Is Dumber

Three off-duty soldiers with girlfriends in the tiny hamlet of Ellensberg, Washington, had already imbibed before picking up their dates. Whether it was the brewskies, the night air, or young love, the soldiers lost all control when they saw a vision above the We-Sak-It-Git-'n-Go shop. There she was, larger than life, and yet so real, so near. She was ten feet off the ground. They gazed up at her with mouths hanging open. She was a fifty-foot-tall, inflatable beer bottle on top of an Ellensberg convenience store.

Like a top-secret mission behind enemy lines, the three silently went to it. Within seconds, they had formed a human ladder and vaulted onto the roof, where they were now positioned to secure the area and take their prisoner. *Poof*! They deflated the bottle and leaped back to the sidewalk, the proud owners of the ultimate

125

party decoration: Paul Bunyan's Bud, the mother of all cold ones.

Just like Privates Moe, Larry, and Curly, they had to blow it up for the guys back at the barrack. The M.P.'s just followed the huge Long Neck in the sky to find them.

It's hard keeping military intelligence bottled up.

A Workman Blames His Tools

William Chase of Putnam, Connecticut, had an ironic tale to tell. It seems his sister and brother-in-law were asleep one summer's eve when a robber came rapping, gently tapping at their window-mounted air conditioner. Chase's brother-in-law is not a small person. When he confronted the burglar, they struggled in the hallway, but the thief managed to wrestle free and get out the back door.

He had gotten in through a window and left a bag on the front steps. Along with the tools in the satchel was the burglar's identification. The truly ironic part: the thief ended up doing time at the very same jail where Chase and his brother-in-law are both correctional officers.

If You Can't Trust a Three-Time Felon, Who Can You Trust?

Back in 1982, Officer Steve Stafford, only three weeks out of the academy, responded to a robbery call at an all-night convenience store in Saraland, Alabama. When the clerk described the getaway car—a blue Toyota mini-van—Officer Stafford recalled passing it. While his backup took the rest of the report, the first officer sped down the street. There at a gas station was the blue mini-van, and two men arguing as they gassed up.

Stafford quickly announced himself as he drew down on the two spatting armed robbers. One of the men started to go for the back of his belt when the officer told him to freeze. Stafford patted the man down and found a .25 caliber pistol in the man's belt. It wasn't loaded—much to the surprise of the crook.

"You sent me in there to rob that place with an empty gun!" this bad guy said to his cohort.

The driver was slightly embarrassed. "Well, I didn't want anybody getting hurt."

"And you forgot to get gas before we rob the place! I don't believe you!"

The driver was very embarrassed. "I know. It was on my list."

The Cop Who Collared Too Much Criminal

New Jersey State Police pride themselves on fitness and speed, but sometimes creativity solves what muscle and sweat cannot.

One evening in a small New Jersey city a drug dealer led two officers on a very short foot chase. You see, this dealer weighed a hair over four hundred pounds. The sprint lasted about half a block. Sweating profusely, the out-of-shape hipster landed all four hundred pounds on the sidewalk. He would not move. Brilliant. The cops eyeballed the huge suspect. The problem with guys like this is that you can't find a good place to grab ahold. Dragging was out of the question.

Then a light bulb came on. The dealing dumbster had plopped down outside a building supply store where a man was moving lumber with a forklift. One officer waved the operator over and asked if he could heft the

Dragging was out of the question.

suspect into his squad car via forklift. "No problem. I got a scoop for fertilizer."

About this time, Jabba the Bubba decided to move on his own rather than getting forklifted out of freedom. He prefers to think of his time in the clinker as a trip to the spa.

A Cowboy and His Boots Are Seldom Parted

Officer Mark Stephanotis of the Marion, Indiana, police department made a routine traffic stop when he clocked a car doing fifty-one in a thirty-five zone. Of course, Mark realized a long time ago that traffic stops are never "routine." For example, more than 70 percent of the drug arrests in the United States result from "routine" traffic stops. This was a simple speeding ticket that took a dramatic turn.

Sure enough, the guy pulled over promptly when he saw Mark's lights, but he also promptly hopped out of his car and bolted on foot. He had a good fifty-yard head start on Mark, and this guy was not slow. When he kicked off his boots, he ran even faster. Mark lost the speedster in the dark residential street, but he knew the guy couldn't have gotten far.

An old lady waved to Mark from a window and pointed to a shed behind her house. Yep, the guy was in the shed, wedged behind a riding lawn mower. He surrendered easily enough, but insisted that he was not the guy Mark had been chasing. He also said that the car was not his, in fact, he'd never seen that car before.

All the way back to the station, the barefoot bad boy insisted that he was not the guy that ran from the car. Mark listened to the familiar and tiresome "I'm not the guy" speech. What can you say, but "Tell it to the judge, pal."

He did tell it to the judge, and he was released on bail pending his trial. Interestingly enough, the same innocent guy was back the next day to claim Mark's only piece of evidence, his cowboy boots.

I Wonder Where That Guy Works

It's about three in the afternoon at a small bar near South Bend, Indiana, when one of the guys at the bar—who's been drinking alone for an hour—is ready to leave. He pulls a gun and demands the cashola. After collecting his money, he strolls out and hops into a car—"Evans Glass Company" painted on the back of it.

He guns the engine and slides on the gravel, slamming into the bar he has just robbed. Now he can't get the car free. Sprinting three blocks, he collapses in a hiding place where no one would even think to look, behind a huge pane of glass—at the Evans Glass Company. That's where the cops found him, oh, a good fifteen minutes later.

Leaping a fence on the embankment, the crook took a tumble
down a hill covered with cactus.

Roll, Tumbleweed, Roll

It was a slow afternoon for Deputy McCracken near Ventura, California, when the call came that a car had been stolen and was headed in his direction. Within moments, Deputy McCracken set up a stakeout. Big as day, there he was, and as soon as he spotted McCracken, he was off to the races.

Before Lead Foot had gone a mile, he had blown his tires. Leaping a fence on the embankment, the crook took a tumble down a hill covered with cactus. At the bottom of the hill was a storm fence, which the bad guy couldn't have cleared on a good day.

So he hiked back up through the cactus to the waiting officers. McCracken was kind enough to take the hedgehog hoodlum to the hospital, where the medical folks removed the cactus spines, one by one.

How well do you know the dumb criminal mind?

A woman in New Orleans was arrested shortly after robbing a small store. Was she caught because . . .

A. She slipped on a dropped fried pie and knocked herself out?

B. While there, she filled out a raffle ticket for a new car?

C. She returned later to buy groceries with the cash?

The correct answer is B. Doesn't she know that losers never win?

It Doesn't Count If I Don't Succeed

The man approaching the customer service desk in a large discount store in Oakland, California, didn't appear to be just another customer making a return. Intuition on our part? Nah. The clue was the paring knife he pointed at the clerk behind the desk. The clerk immediately picked up the phone and called security. Before she could get a word out, the man dropped the knife, ran to the parking lot, and left in his car.

Only an hour later, the same man again approached the customer service desk. Unarmed this time, he had a simple request: "Can I have my paring knife back? My wife will kill me if I break up that set of knives."

Real sharp.

The bull rhino hit the door going full steam. *Crash!* Door 1, Dummy 0.

The Bigger They Are, the Harder the Door

Officers use every trick in the book when it comes to taking control of someone who doesn't like the idea of being controlled. Here's another from that bag of tricks.

An off-duty officer in Las Vegas was working store security one night when a large college student shoplifted a pint of gin. Detectives met the shoplifter at the front of the store. A peaceful solution was not to be. The huge student ducked his head like an interior lineman on the football squad and barreled toward the only exit not covered by a store detective—the exit was locked.

The bull rhino hit the door going full steam. *Crash*! Door 1, Dummy 0.

A Buddy Story about Mac and Pepe

Mac was a professional break-in artist who specialized in suburban residences such as, say, Dermont Hill, Illinois. He was a fastidiously neat and nonviolent person, who happened to prefer taking other people's belongings to actually working and earning money himself.

This was to be his most memorable job. The house was clear. No one was at home. Mac entered without the slightest delay through a partially locked sliding glass door. Then he met Pepe, a Chihuahua weighing in at about nine pounds. Pepe was a fairly laid-back pooch, so it only took Mac a minute or two to make friends and go about his business.

The consummate professional, Mac checked the family calendar in the kitchen. Much to Mac's delight, the family was on vacation for four days!

Mac and Pepe lived it up, enjoying the hot tub with iced drinks, bathing, and watching television. Heck, Mac even ordered pizza and forged a family check. On the morning of the third day, Mac was showering and heard something. Dripping wet, he stepped out into the hallway. That's when Mac dropped the soap. At that moment, Pepe began barking loudly and startled Mac. Mac slipped on the soap and down the hardwood hallway floor he slid until he stopped abruptly, his head wedged between two posts on the railing of the stairway.

Mac squirmed and pushed, but to no avail. There he was, naked, damp, and very stuck. Of course, Pepe couldn't resist tormenting his new captive in creative and unsanitary ways. For almost forty-eight hours, Mac took Pepe's abuse until the family returned. They stopped laughing long enough to call the police.

A Blonde with a Conscience

Officer Wayne Strain out of Springfield, Missouri, re-members being out patrolling one quiet Friday night, when a pizza delivery guy flagged him down. Strain assumed the young man had been robbed, but it wasn't quite that simple.

The pizza guy explained that, on the previous Friday, they had received a call for a delivery to a nearby high-rise apartment building. When the delivery boy knocked at the apartment, he was told in no uncertain terms that no one there had ordered a pizza. Returning to his vehicle, he found three other pizzas missing.

Strain couldn't understand why the kid flagged him down to report a week-old pizza theft, but the kid went on. His pizza joint had just received another order to the same apartment building, from a woman with the same voice. Strain went along with the junior pizza sleuth and staked out his car while he delivered.

Seconds after the delivery guy went into the lobby, a

When he confronted the blonde, she dropped the pizzas at Wayne's feet and came clean.

145

beautiful blonde appeared out of the bushes and jumped into the pizza car. She grabbed a couple of large pizzas and headed around the corner. Strain happened to be behind that very corner. When he confronted the blonde, she dropped the pizzas at Wayne's feet and came clean.

"I didn't steal any pizza last Friday. I swear to God. I didn't steal any pizza last Friday night."

Those Darn Trick-or-Treaters

63

The dispatcher in Many, Louisiana, received a call from a citizen complaining of the marijuana smoke billowing from their neighbor's apartment. The police responded to the address, and officer Dean Lambert approached the front door while his partner went to cover the back.

Lambert knocked a little too soon—his partner was not yet in place at the back door. He could hear scurrying around inside after he announced himself, and his partner was almost hit in the face by a paper sack the suspect tossed out a back window. Finally, the suspect opened the front door as innocently as any law-abiding citizen.

Lambert explained why he was there and asked if he could search the man's apartment.

"No problem. There are no drugs in my house. Never have been and never will be."

Peering around, Lambert spotted a paper bag on the kitchen table and walked over to inspect the contents. It was half-filled with marijuana.

"Well, then, what's this?" Lambert asked, looking down in the bag at the marijuana.

"Oh, that's just some candy I got for the little trick-or-treaters."

That's when Lambert's backup came in through the back door, holding the paper bag the man had tossed into the backyard.

"Hey, thanks for the candy." Then Lambert cuffed him.

Yo Quiero Jail Time

It was a Friday lunch hour in Milwaukee when a man entered a Taco Bell and took a place in line. It was the lunch rush, so about thirty or forty people had gathered behind the man by the time he finally reached the counter. That's when he pulled a gun and announced, "This is a holdup."

Behind him, he heard metal sliding against leather and voices saying, "No, it's not." He slowly turned, only to face twenty-three weapons drawn, aimed at his head and chest.

It so happens this Taco Bell was located about a block from the Milwaukee Police Academy, where a conference for officers from around the state had just taken a lunch break.

Door-to-Door Salesman

We're all familiar with the old phrase "seeing double." Leave it up to one of America's dumbest criminals to come up with a new term, "seeing triple."

Our story begins in Utica, New York, where a lone policeman responded to a burglary call at a local car dealership. As the officer got out of his patrol car, he saw what appeared to be a flashlight shining on the inside of the building. Cautiously making his way to the wall, he peered in through the small window of a side door. Inside he saw the perpetrator looking right back at him.

As their eyes met, the man inside suddenly bolted to another door in an effort to escape. The officer quickly ran to the same door. They met again. Not ready to capitulate just yet, the man opted for the third and final door, arriving just in time to face the same officer.

Realizing the futility of it all, the man threw his arms into the air in disgust and blurted, "I give up, you have the place surrounded!" And with that, the officer placed the out-of-work salesman under arrest.

Outnumbered? Nah. Outsmarted.

Counter Space ... Cadet

People don't plan to fail, they fail to plan. Well, this guy in Illinois did neither . . . but he failed anyway.

One November day in Des Plaines, Illinois, snow was falling. Construction work was over for the year, and Bobby James wasn't looking forward to a long, cold winter with no money.

James had a plan. He would rob the gas station a few miles away from his house—maybe even two or three places—and, if everything went smoothly, he would spend the winter in Florida. James wasn't stupid like those other criminals that he had seen on TV. Those guys got caught because they didn't think it through. James remembered one robber who carried his wallet in his back pocket, only to leave it lying on the floor when he decided to use the bathroom. Well, that wasn't going to happen to him.

First off, he wasn't taking the money bag with him. He'd bring along a re-sealable plastic bag to carry the bills. Fingerprints? Gloves would take care of that. And the wallet? Well, he'd carry his ID with him in case he got pulled over. But in his front pocket. He would use the bathroom *before* he headed out on his mission.

So far, so good. He loitered around the magazine rack inside the gas station until the last customer walked out. In a flash, he made his move. Armed with a razor knife, he demanded all the money in the cash drawer from the frightened clerk. The shaking cashier quickly grabbed two fistfuls of greenbacks and laid them on the counter in front of the thief.

Out of habit, but at any rate the clerk asked, "Would you like a bag for that?"

"I brought my own bag, just put the money right in the—." He stopped in midsentence. Where was the bag that he'd brought? Oh yeah, in his front right pocket. After removing some papers, a few dollars, and his wallet from his pocket to get the baggie, he deposited them in a pile on the counter. Scooping up the money, he swiftly dropped it into the plastic bag and ran from the store.

Ever get that feeling that you forgot something? Bobby James did, but it was too late. Before his adrenaline stopped pumping and his vital signs returned to normal, the police were already on their way to return his wallet.

. . . Now Weaving on Runway 31

Here's a classic example of what happens when an understanding cop meets an honest drunk driver.

In the military as a law enforcement officer for the air force at Norton Air Force Base in California, Rex Brocki was on duty one night when he spotted a civilian car driving on the base. It didn't take Sherlock Holmes to realize the male driver was quite intoxicated. Why else would someone be driving his car at night down the runway, where C-141 cargo planes landed?

Behind the weaving suspect's car, the officer called in the tag number for "wants and warrants." That done, Officer Brocki "lit him up" with his blue lights. The man drifted toward the right side of the runway, then slowly weaved back left to the yellow line. He weaved all the way to the right again, then drifted back to the yellow line, and weaved over to the right once more. Finally, he just stopped dead on the runway.

Brocki exited his vehicle and approached the discombobulated driver, who had already exited his car. Having heard it all before, the officer wondered what lame excuse the driver was about to lay on him. Before the officer could speak, however, the bewildered drunk raised his palms and slurred in earnest, "Officer, I saw your lights, I wanted to pull over. I just couldn't find the curb!"

The veteran officer, who had heard it all, found the man's honesty quite refreshing. So instead of a ride to jail, the man was given a safe ride home.

It's "plane" to see that honesty is the best policy.

How well do you know the dumb criminal mind?

A young carjacker was caught and arrested by police within twenty minutes of his theft. Was it because . . .

A. He drove the victim home to get the title and registration?
B. The vehicle was equipped with the LoJack tracking system?
C. He wasn't aware he'd stolen a stolen car the police were already looking for?

The correct answer is A. During the carjacking, the owner convinced the thief to drive him home to get the title and registration. Once home, he phoned the police.

Disorder in the Court

While talking with another officer working security at the courthouse in Des Moines, Washington, Officer Steve Lettic watched with casual interest as the man about to pass through the metal detector emptied the contents of his pockets into the plastic bowl. Along with the usual keys, coins, and nail clippers, a plastic bag of off-colored rocks was tossed in as well. The baggie no sooner hit the bowl than the man snatched it back up and stuffed it in his pocket. Acting as though nothing had happened, he proceeded down the hallway and into a courtroom.

He was quick, but not quick enough. Both officers had seen the baggie of rock cocaine. After a brief powwow, the officer on duty walked down to the courtroom and instructed the individual to come back out. Just as the man got to the door, he reached into his pocket and threw the baggie into a corner. A plainclothes officer saw this and thought the guy was littering, so he told him to pick it up.

For the second time in less than five minutes, the man grabbed the baggie and now rushed past the officer standing at the door. Zigging and zagging his way past Officer Lettic, he ran from the courthouse, only to be captured within a block.

Upon the man's arrest, a subsequent search of his person turned up fifteen hundred dollars in cash, along with a pager. The baggie containing the crack was found on the roof of a nearby house. He was arrested and charged with possession of narcotics. His money was seized as proceeds from drug sales.

No doubt: The next time he entered a courtroom, it wasn't as a spectator.

Have Gun, Will Travel

Many years ago, when Sheriff Loren Brand of Panhandle, Texas, was still a rookie, he encountered a dumb criminal who had to make a quick decision. Luckily for the quicker-thinking sheriff, it was the wrong one.

It all began one afternoon while Sheriff Brand walked his beat. As the officer was about to pass an open entrance to a building, he heard hurried footsteps coming down a flight of stairs to his right, with shouts of "*Stop! Thief!*" echoing above him. A man bolted out of the building and took off sprinting down the sidewalk. The young rookie gave chase.

In those days, Brand carried what he describes as "an old .38 revolver in a well-worn, hand-me-down swivel holster." At warp speed, he was closing the gap on the burglary suspect. All of a sudden, his revolver jumped from its holster and went skittering down the sidewalk in front of him. Unable to slow down, the officer accidentally kicked the weapon and sent it speeding

159

The officer accidentally kicked the weapon and sent it speeding toward the fleeing suspect, striking him in the back of his ankle.

160

toward the fleeing suspect, striking him in the back of his ankle.

The man turned, saw the weapon, and began to reach for it. In a no-nonsense voice, the heavily panting officer pointed his finger at the suspect and said, "Reach for that weapon and I'll shoot you!" The suspect stepped back from the loaded .38 and placed his hands over his head. Brand picked up his gun and placed the man under arrest.

Brand was thankful that the man was just as good a thinker as he was a burglar, or Brand might never have gotten the chance to tell us this story.

70 **Taxi Cabin**

Patrol Commander Steve Bowers of the sheriff's department in Boise, Idaho, had the pleasure of arresting this dumb guy shortly after it appeared he'd gotten away.

It was early on a Saturday evening when the police station received a call. A woman living in a remote area had been robbed by her old boyfriend. He'd broken into her mountain cabin home, then robbed and threatened her. Commander Bowers responded to the call.

When Bowers arrived at the scene, the woman verified the facts and gave him the man's name and address. She told him the ex-boyfriend had left on foot not more than twenty minutes earlier.

Bowers called for assistance. With the help of two officers, Bowers began a sweep of the area. When an hour's search turned up nothing, Bowers decided, for the safety of all concerned, to call off the manhunt for the night. The mountain terrain was rugged and darkness was setting in.

As the law officers discussed resuming the search the next day, a call came in from dispatch.

"Is the person you're looking for named Zeke Kane?" the dispatcher inquired.

"Yes, it is," Bowers responded.

"Well, I just received a call from the dispatcher of a taxi service, who said that a 'Zeke Kane' had just called for a cab at the J&L Tavern, and he had told them to make it fast because 'the cops are after me!' "

Officer Bowers smiled. "Tell them to cancel the taxi. I'll be picking up Mr. Kane at the J&L myself."

With another officer along as support, Bowers went to the location and found the suspect hiding in the bushes, waiting for his taxi. He was charged with the crime, no charge for the ride.

An Open and Clothed Case

Duty du jour for Deputy Greg Deivert in Oregon was to transport inmates from the county jail to the courthouse for appearances. One inmate scheduled for trial was up on a stolen car charge. As the deputy waited for him to get dressed, the man held up two shirts and studied them. "There's really not a lot to think about, I guess; I've only got two shirts anyway," he said out loud. Choosing the old U.S. Navy shirt, he pulled it on.

The victim told the jury that, on the morning in question, he arrived at work on the construction site where he was a foreman. As he was closing his car's trunk, he looked over at the car parked beside him and saw a young man. The victim said that the man waved at him as he walked by. Approximately fifteen minutes later, he returned to his car for some blueprints, and it was gone. That was four months ago.

The district attorney then said, "Please look at the

young man seated at the defendant's table and tell the court if this is the man who waved to you that morning."

The victim hesitated, then asked the defendant to stand. He studied him for a moment and said, "Yes sir, that's him."

The defense attorney went volcanic. "*Wait a minute!*" he shouted. "Do you honestly expect this court to believe that you can positively identify a man that, by your own testimony, you saw for no longer than ten seconds, four months ago?"

The victim answered, "If you look real close at the shirt he's wearing, you'll see my name under the navy insignia. That shirt was in the trunk of my car!"

The courtroom exploded with laughter, the defense attorney collapsed into his chair, and the prosecution rested. The judge pronounced the defendant guilty.

"The clothes make the man." In this case, they also make him guilty.

 **Wingnut**

One day during Officer Dennis Gillum's stint as a police officer at Plattsburgh Air Force Base in upstate New York, the base exchange (BX) was robbed of more than fifty thousand dollars. The description of the thief was ambiguous, and according to Officer Gillum, he "left no fingerprints, and no one saw which way he fled."

Well, you gotta know something went wrong or Mister Mastermind wouldn't be in this book. But what could it be? He'd already gotten away with it. Three weeks after the robbery, Gillum received a phone call from a local car-dealership owner. Someone from the base had strutted into the showroom, picked out a new car, and paid cash for it. The bills were stacks of tens and twenties, still neatly wrapped in paper bands bearing the BX logo.

Busted!

An Alarming Realization

73

People with guilty consciences do things to give themselves away. Let's again head East, where a shoplifter captured herself.

As is the case at most retail stores, merchandise at Norton's Department Store in Lakehurst, New Jersey, is tagged with those pesky security clips that trip the alarm if the clerk hasn't deactivated them at the checkout counter. A woman had just purchased some clothing and was passing through the exit door at about the same time as another woman, who wasn't carrying anything. The alarm was triggered, and strident beeping filled the air.

The smiling store manager and the security guard at the door had seen the first woman pay for the articles and knew the clerk had merely forgotten to deactivate the tags. But before either had a chance to speak, the woman standing next to her began pulling out several skirts and blouses from beneath her bulky clothing. She

The alarm was triggered, and strident beeping filled the air.

was detained by the officer and manager until the authorities arrived to take her to jail.

The real kicker came when she was taken to the manager's office, and it was discovered that none of the clothing she was stealing had any security tags on 'em!

So clothes, and yet so far away.

Going Up . . . Going Down . . . Going to Jail

They say, "Everything's big in Texas." And that's pretty true, as long as you ignore this guy's brain-cell count.

Our story opens with a call to the police department in Sherman, Texas. A tattooed man was roaming the parking lot of a nearby truck stop, offering to sell "speed" to over-the-road truckers.

Deputy Sheriff B. A. Mitchell took the call and, within a few minutes, he was on the scene scouting the parking lot in his patrol car. As Mitchell was cruising the lot, he noticed a man who fit the description given the officer. Sheriff Mitchell pulled up beside him and got out of his car.

"Afternoon, sir. Can I see some ID?"

"Why you hassling me, man?" came the confrontational response.

As the suspect had set the tone of the interview, the

sheriff got right to the point. "We received a call that you were trying to sell speed to the truckers out here."

The guy shook his head and laughed out loud. "You guys are so stupid!" He opened his hand to reveal over a dozen pills in his palm. "These ain't speed, man; they're downers!"

He was arrested and charged with drug possession with intent to sell.

Talk about downers.

 **Canadummies**

Our good friends up in Canada often chip in with some great material for America's Dumbest Criminals, and while this book is geared toward the good ol' U.S. of A., we decided to sneak this one past our publisher. It's too good to leave out.

The details on this story are a little sketchy, but the gist of it is about a man and his girlfriend who robbed three banks in the span of an hour in the Vancouver area. They were driven to each bank by their unwitting landlady, who thought she was merely giving them a ride to pick up some past-due rent money. The landlady had no idea what was going on.

After the third robbery, the threesome went back to the couple's house. The boyfriend and the landlady went their separate ways, and the girlfriend went inside.

Unaware that she had been followed home by two employees of the last bank job (she lived across the street from the third bank), the girlfriend was still shaking from all the excitement when the police fitted her for matching bracelets. A moment later the phone rang. One of the officers answered. It was the woman's boyfriend. In an attempt to lure the guy back over to the house, the policeman told the guy he was her new boyfriend and not to call her anymore.

The guy might have been an idiot, but he was no fool. He called 911 to tell the police there was a burglar in his girlfriend's house. They traced the call and he was picked up shortly thereafter.

Which goes to show, dumb knows no boundaries.

Shake, Rattle, and Parole

Mark Moffett, a policeman in Huntington Beach, California, was the first to arrive on the scene of a restaurant that had just been robbed. The cashier told Moffett that, around nine o'clock, a man walked in, pressed a gun to her head, and emptied the cash register of about two hundred dollars.

Writing down the details of the robbery, Officer Moffett asked her if she could describe the armed gunman.

"Sure," she said. "He's my neighbor!"

"The guy who just robbed you is your neighbor?" Moffett asked incredulously.

"Yeah. His name is Terry." Pointing to an apartment building a hundred yards from where they were standing, she added, "You see those apartments right there? That's where I live, in apartment ten. Terry lives with his girlfriend across the hall from me in apartment eleven."

"And you're positive that this 'Terry' guy is the one who robbed you?" Officer Moffett asked.

"Absolutely. I see him every day."

Still wondering if it were possible for anyone to be that dumb, Moffett, along with backup, entered the apartment building and knocked on the door of apartment eleven. A young woman answered.

"Where's Terry?" Moffett demanded.

"He's in the back bedroom," the rattled woman replied.

Sure enough, when the officers opened the closet door, there sat Terry still clutching the gun and the money. As it turned out, he had been paroled from prison only a week earlier—for robbery! The arrest is history.

Armward and Upward

The man on the witness stand in New Orleans was in obvious pain. Moving his right arm ever so slightly caused him to wince. The attorney for the insurance company sat at one table. The man's attorney sat at the other.

The case was solid. The man had injured his arm six months earlier in a job-related accident. He was suing the insurance company of his former employer for permanent disability.

The injury wasn't disputed, but the permanency was. After a series of questions that his client answered perfectly, the man's lawyer had one final question. With the smug look of victory on his face, he asked the clincher, "How high can you raise your arm right now?"

Straining, the man slowly lifted his outstretched arm to shoulder level.

"Fine," his attorney nodded sympathetically. "And how far could you lift it before the accident?" Without hesitation, the man proudly shot the same arm straight above his head exclaiming, "This high!" He was still holding his arm up when the judge slammed down his gavel and announced, "Case dismissed!"

The arm works fine. Obviously it was the brain that sustained the real damage.

How well do you know the dumb criminal mind?

A strange man in Greeley, Colorado, was dismissed by the court as a potential juror. Was it because . . .

A. He wore a black hood with a noose around his neck and carried a double bladed ax to court?
B. He was the Siamese twin of the accused?
C. When asked to state his name he replied, "Gill T. Asell"?

The correct answer is A, lending new meaning to the term "dressed to kill."

Bushted

An officer in Cudahy, Wisconsin, was in hot pursuit, on foot, of a suspected burglar. After a two-block chase, he found the man crouched in some shrubbery in front of a house.

"What are you doing in there?" the officer asked him.

"Oh, hi. I locked myself out of the house and I'm looking for the spare key I keep out here in the bushes," the man told him.

"That's strange," the officer said. "Why would you do that?"

"In case I lock myself out, I told you."

"Oh, I *know* why you'd hide an extra key," the amused officer responded. "I just want to know why you would hide it at *my* house!"

As with real estate, the *key* to this story is location, location, location.

179

79 He's Got a Ticket to Hide

If you run a business, you know that good help is hard to find these days. But there seems to be no shortage of dumb help.

The manager of an appliance-electronics and jewelry rental store in Austin, Texas, was phoned on a Sunday by the store's alarm company and told his store had been broken into. The manager was expecting to find the typical shattered window or smashed-in door, but at the scene he was surprised to see no broken glass and the officer still sitting in his patrol car.

"Your front door is open," the responding officer informed him. Both men entered the store to find everything still in order. All the display cases were still locked, and nothing appeared to be missing.

"Do you have a safe?" the cop asked.

"Yes, in the back of the store. I'll show you."

Walking into his office, the manager gasped. There

stood the safe with the door wide open. All the jewelry placed there for safekeeping had been wiped out.

Come Monday afternoon, the store manager was contacted by two Austin detectives. Some of the jewelry had been located at a local pawn shop. Once at the store, he made the positive ID and examined the pawn tickets issued for the gems. The signature on the pawn tickets was that of an employee.

There you have it: A looter low enough to steal from his employer, yet dumb enough to sign his real name on the pawn tickets. The manager thanked the detectives and returned to his store, where he received another phone call. This time it was from the thieving employee, calling to say he wouldn't be in to work—he was sick. But since it was payday, he wondered what time his check might be ready. He was told to come on in at two o'clock and his check would be waiting for him. The manager then phoned the detectives. They would be waiting, too.

The two plainclothes detectives were posing as customers when the employee entered the store to get his paycheck. They came up behind him as he stood at the counter and placed him under arrest.

"What's this all about?" he asked, acting surprised.

"Robbery," he was told by the detectives. While one read him his rights, the other detective began removing articles from the man's pockets. They opened his wallet to discover five pawn tickets for jewelry. A search of his vehicle produced three more tickets—all with his name on them. The employee, that is, ex-employee, had no further questions.

There was no one else to blame for his wanton stupidity. He "ticket a pawn himself" to be an idiot.

Ahhh . . . Baloney

Here's a tale about a sport diver whose good luck went out with the tide.

It had been a good day for Jerry Crain in sunny California. He'd only been diving for a few hours and had already filled two burlap bags with abalone. One bagful was within the strict limits set by the local fish and game department, while the over-the-limit other was stuffed with undersized abalone, a double legal no-no.

California fish and game warden John Dymek had been watching the diver from the cliffs above with a pair of high-powered field binoculars. He knew that at least half of the diver's "catch of the day" was in violation of California law because of the one-bag limit.

Dymek watched as the loaded-down diver began his ascent up the steep hills above the beach. It wasn't an easy climb. The ground was soft and sandy and the footing loose.

The loaded-down diver began his ascent up the steep hills above
the beach. It wasn't an easy climb.

184

He was still catching his breath when he heard someone approaching—Dymek, in uniform. Without a word, the diver picked up one of the sacks of abalone and, like an Olympian hammer thrower, began spinning in circles, swinging the sack in circular gyrations above his head. With one loud grunt, he sent it flying over the cliffs to the ocean below. Almost. By now the evening tide had rolled out, and the bag landed solidly on the dry tide bed a good ten yards from the water.

If that weren't dumb enough, when the officer checked out the contents of the unthrown bag, he discovered that "lNeptune" had dropped the bag containing the undersized abalone; the diver had hurled the bag with the *legal catch over the cliff.*

According to Warden Dymek, "The discarded bag was recovered, and the poacher was also charged with, and convicted of, attempting to destroy evidence."

Surfs him right!

Legally Blind Justice

Here's a first: A guy whose disguise actually *gave him away.*

Our story starts with an armed robbery of a pizza parlor in Sparks, Nevada. When Officer Robert J. Fuller arrived on the scene, he was told by the manager that a tall man with pantyhose pulled down over his face had entered the store, pulled out a gun, and forced him to give up the day's proceeds. But the robber had cut only one eyehole out of the pantyhose. The right eye. In fact, the hole was so large, the manager could see the entire right side of the perpetrator's face. Officer Fuller filled out his report and left the store.

Fuller knew of a man who had several arrests on his record and lived only two blocks from the pizza parlor. The man was blind in his left eye. *Was it possible,* the officer thought to himself, *that the suspect would be so dumb as to cut out only one eyehole in the pantyhose before robbing the store?* It was. During a field lineup a few days later, the man was positively identified.

On the day of his jury trial, the accused entered the courtroom with his attorney. He carried a white cane and wore dark glasses. He feebly tapped his way between the rows of spectators on the way to his table and bumped into several pieces of furniture.

The defense attorney addressed the jury. "How could my client possibly be the perpetrator, when he is recognized as legally blind by the state of Nevada?"

Leave it to the prosecutor to fill in the blank. He produced a police report showing that, while out on bail for the robbery, the accused had received his second DUI! He was found guilty and sentenced to prison.

For all concerned, this case was a real eye-opener.

How well do you know the dumb criminal mind?

A recently fired employee who'd gotten away clean with burglarizing his former boss's business was caught by the police when they discovered that . . .

A. While participating in a televised psychic experiment, he was told to write down something that only he would know?

B. The piece of paper he'd used to prop the door open during his burglary was a speeding ticket he'd gotten a week earlier?

C. Although he disguised his voice, he used his home phone when he called the boss back to brag about the crime, and the office had caller ID?

The correct answer is B. Take this job and ticket!

Mobile Home Boy

Well, after nearly two months of being a "monitor zombie," I was taking a break when I told Daniel a funny story of a friend of mine who had had a run-in with the law. Daniel laughed and said, "Hey, you've got only one more story to write, put *that* one in there." So here it is.

You'd have to know Bolty Boy and his gypsy-type lifestyle to fully appreciate his character and quick wit. Down on his luck, he maintains a minstrel's heart and finds humor in whatever comes his way, good or bad.

Back in the late seventies, Bolty drove a mid-sixties Pontiac Lemans. He also lived in it. I used to refer to it as the Pontiac Apartments. When the car was running, he'd pull into a gas station about every eight miles and drive up to the full-service pump.

"Check the oil and fluff the pillows," he'd say with the air of an aristocrat. After dispensing three dollars' worth of gas, the frustrated attendant spent the next thirty minutes tightening bolts, replacing hoses, and responding to

Bolty's interrogation: everything from oil leaks to slipping transmissions. Bolty was financially challenged, and he relished any free advice he could get.

One time Bolty and I were going out Hillsboro Road in Nashville, Tennessee, when I suggested to him that he could afford to get a real place to live with all the money it was costing him to maintain his car-apartment. He really did need a place with more room, and I suggested something along the line of a Buick or Chrysler.

We both started laughing, when the cop's siren wailing behind us jolted Bolty. He pulled over. We were still chuckling when the police officer reached the window.

"Afternoon, sir," he said. "The reason I stopped you is that the speed limit through here is thirty-five, and I clocked you at fifty-one miles an hour."

Bolty stiffened noticeably in his seat. "Fifty-one miles an hour?" he muttered. "That's impossible, officer! This car won't *run* an hour!"

The cop thought it was pretty funny, too. He let him off with a warning and a smile.

Even Cowboys Get the Blues

Working undercover narcotics in long hair and a mustache, Officer Chuck Warner of Craig, Colorado, was grabbing a cold drink at a local convenience store one night, when he was approached by a man he described as a "dirty-looking cowboy." He asked Warner which way he was headed; he needed a ride. With some time to kill, Warner agreed to give him a lift.

The man introduced himself as "Cowboy Bob," throwing his gear into the unmarked car. Bob was quite a talker. In no time, he was telling his life story. Then the conversation shifted to the police. Bob began to talk about the local cops and how dumb they all were. He patted his shirt pocket. "Yep," he sighed. "Twenty-seven years of smokin' dope and never busted."

In the middle of another babble, Bob suddenly grew quiet. Several moments of silence passed before Officer Warner looked up. Cowboy Bob's gaze was fixed on the center console. He was staring at the police radio . . . and the handcuffs . . . and the pepper spray. His eyes began drifting slowly around the squad car while his head remained frozen in place. They came to rest on the shotgun.

Cowboy Bob then deftly lifted the corner of the small satchel he'd tossed onto the dashboard as he got in. He'd discovered the blue and red dash light under the bag. His voice cracked, "Chuck, whatcha do for a living?" he stammered.

Officer Warner smiled and said, "Bob, you can't be that dumb."

"Oh, yes, I can," he gulped.

Well Cowboy "Boob" was right. The dope in the shirt (Bob) was taken down to the police station, along with the dope in his pocket. It'll be a while before Cowboy Bob's back in the saddle.

I'm a Criminal Trainee—Please Bear with Me

84

Job orientation is a time-consuming and difficult task for anyone, but especially for criminals and bank tellers. When a criminal trainee and a bank trainee cross paths, the results can be time-consuming and hilarious.

Two would-be bank robbers were completing their on-the-job training by pulling a bank heist in Virginia Beach, Virginia. They carefully followed step one: case the area and make sure there are no police officers around. Check.

Step two: Approach the bank in a normal manner, and mentally note your escape route. Check and check.

Step three: Put on a mask, remember the bag for the money, and enter the bank with confidence. Check. Check. Check.

Step four: Approach the first teller you see, and ask her to put all the money in the bag. Check.

This is our trainee-meets-trainee moment.

"I'm sorry, sir. This is not my window," the bank teller

trainee responded. "I was just getting some more deposit slips for my window."

Uh-oh. This wasn't covered in the criminal trainee's training program.

"Well, uh, take me to your window and get the money from your window," one of the robbers intoned. (Aha, problem-solving skills are a must in a good criminal—give 'im two points.)

"I'm the drive-through teller today, sir, and this is only my third day," the courteous teller countered, still sticking to bank policy by the letter. "You'll have to drive through in a car." Good Trainee.

"Well, uh, can't you just open the door and take me back there?" Credit him with another few points.

"I can't, sir. I'm sorry. They haven't given me the code to open the doors yet." She's cooperating with the robber as best she can, which is bank policy. It's also bank procedure to hit the silent alarm, which she did as she spoke.

The criminal trainee mulled the situation over a bit and then started to run out of the bank, only to remember that he had left his backpack back on the counter. Subtract five points for leaving his personal belongings at the scene, but add ten points for remembering.

The criminal trainee jumps in the getaway car and the driver guns the motor. Remembering not to draw attention to themselves, they immediately slow down to the same speed as the traffic around them. Add five points.

Surrounded by squad cars and officers with guns drawn, the criminal trainees put their hands in the air and surrendered. Give these guys, oh, twenty-five points, er, years. The final tally from the judges: bank trainee, 100 points; criminal trainees, minus 45 points. No contest.

Crocodile Dumbdee

The man entering a Miami courtroom for arraignment strutted down the aisle, his arms out to his side, and exclaimed to the judge, "Your honor, I know what the allegations are, but who are the *allegators*?"

The Age of Asparagus

Here's a man who confuses his legal rights with a popular musical group from the seventies.

One Friday night, Officer Jack Dedmon was booking a "hippie-looking" burglary suspect in Fresno, California. The space cadet was cooperative until Officer Dedmon attempted to fingerprint him.

"I know my rights, man!" he protested loudly. *"I don't have to let you take my fingerprints!"*

Okay, the guy wasn't the sharpest knife in the drawer, but he did have to be printed.

"I know my rights and I don't have to!" he shouted.

Dedmon was puzzled. "Why won't you let me take your fingerprints?"

"Because my mama told me I didn't have to, and I'm standin' on the fifth dimension!"

Obviously.

87 Pedal into the Metal

ATF Officer Bill Kingman and a partner were working undercover, making drug buys in a high-crime neighborhood in Louisiana. The regular dealers spotted the undercover guys cruising in their late model Chevy after a few passes, but the lesser-experienced dealers went for it.

"We had a takedown car that was just up the block from us," Kingman recalls. "We would make the buy in plain view of the takedown car. We'd radioed those guys and they would pursue and apprehend the dealer. That's how it's supposed to work. But when this clown came up to my window on a bicycle, things got weird."

The dealer on the two-wheeler showed Kingman some crack cocaine, and Bill quickly came up with the cash. In a twinkling of the eye, the deal was done. The crack cycler began to pull away, and Bill grabbed the radio. While Kingman gave the takedown car the dealer's description, his partner started to pull away from the curb.

The dealer was free-wheeling down the street and kept looking over his shoulder at Kingman and his partner—he thought they were following him. Actually, they just wanted to pass him and leave the scene. The faster they went, the faster the pusher pedaled, always looking back over his shoulder. Before Kingman could finish radioing the necessary information, *wham,* the dealer smacked into the back of the takedown car.

"My last line to the takedown guys," Kingman said, "was 'It's that guy lying face down on your back window.' We all laughed for a good five minutes."

88 Dog Day Afternoon

That old saying "Don't believe everything you hear" applies nicely to this story.

Pennsylvania police officer Stephen Alcorn responded to a call of two men fighting in a bar one afternoon. After he arrived at the scene, Officer Alcorn spotted the two still pushing and shoving one another in front of the tavern.

Seeing the cop, one of the men took off running across a small field adjacent to the tavern. Officer Alcorn took the access road around the field and positioned his squad car to intercept the fleeing man. The weeds were shoulder high and only the man's bobbing head was visible. The man screeched to a halt fifty feet away and ducked below the top of the overgrowth.

"Hey!" Alcorn yelled to him, "you're not goin' to get away, so why don't you just come on out?"

"Forget you!" the man yelled back.

Officer Alcorn shook his head as he reached inside his

pocket and pulled out his keys. He began to shake them vigorously. "C'mon, boy!" he said. "Let's get him!"

The man's head quickly popped up over the weeds.

"If you don't come out right now, buddy, I'm sending the K-9 unit in," Alcorn said, still rattling the keys.

As another squad car pulled up next to Officer Alcorn's, the man saw the futility of his situation. "All right! All right!" he shouted back. "I'm comin' out. Just keep that dog away from me."

The man walked out of the field and Officer Alcorn placed him under arrest without incident. In the police car, he turned to the cop and said, "Hey, where's that dog?"

Doggone, that was a great idea.

 **89**

Like a Duck on a Pond

Let's go north of the border to Dalhousie, Ontario, for another crime with a happy ending, starring a young man who stole a mountain bike—in broad daylight, downtown.

The daring young Dalhousian grabbed the bike from a store display and pedaled off down an alley—that dead-ended into a community police station parking lot. Now, you see where this is going, even if the bicyclist didn't. An officer just pulling in didn't see the frantic felon. The kid, thinking he was about to be cornered, ditched the bike and dove into a pond. He swam for his life to the other side to avoid capture. (Remember, no one is chasing him yet.)

Exhausted and dripping wet, the dumb creature from the black lagoon emerged at the very moment another officer was pulling into an adjoining fast food restaurant for lunch. Likewise, he didn't notice the walking pond scum. Still, our harried anti-hero was convinced a SWAT

The kid, thinking he was about to be cornered, ditched the bike and dove into a pond.

team of cops was closing in on him. He dove back into the pond. Gasping for air, he dragged himself out again and ran for freedom. He burst onto the street and ran right into, yep, another squad car.

The officer could barely understand the soggy suspect's weeping confession as he gave himself up to a third cop who wasn't looking for him and had no idea what he was talking about. Wet behind the ears.

Stomp in the Name of the Law

Every year around the middle of summer, the Tennessee skies are abuzz with the sound of Drug Task Force helicopters in search of marijuana crops. On this particular afternoon, the pilot radioed he had located some plants growing on a commercial farm.

The police knew, considering the easy access to the area, it would be nearly impossible to prove who the grower might be. As the chopper was hovering above the pot, a man came running out of a nearby barn and began stomping down the plants, one by one.

Since the man knew the location of every plant, it was pretty safe to assume he was the grower. He was arrested and charged.

Stalling For Time

It was a typically crowded league night at the Fair Lanes Bowling Center in Chandler, Arizona. Al Bacon, a Chandler police officer and a bowler on the police team—with a 160 average—took a break in the men's room.

Bacon was off duty, having fun, but he never turned off his observant detective mind. He immediately noticed four sets of legs occupying two men's stalls. Bacon leaned back and watched.

"Okay, Donny, you get the Walkman." An arm reached over one stall wall, with a Walkman still in its packaging. Another hand reached up and grabbed it from stall number two. Bacon could hear the packaging being ripped off, and then saw it hit the floor.

This restroom gift exchange went back and forth with CDs, batteries, and baseball cards changing hands. Bacon watched quietly until the stall doors finally opened. The four boys carried backpacks and greeted Bacon with stunned looks when he introduced himself. You could've heard a pin drop.

The brilliant potty partners had just shoplifted more than four hundred dollars' worth of merchandise from the discount store across the street. They had picked the bowling alley restroom stalls as a convenient place to divvy up their loot.

That night, the four members of Chandler's police bowling team went home with one win for the team, one collar apiece.

The Dumb Criminal Foreign Exchange Service

Dumb crime is like American Express for some folks: They never leave home without it. That was certainly true for two American lads who went north to see the beautiful scenery of British Columbia, Canada.

The Canadian viewing audience met two down-on-their-luck Yanks on the evening news, when the local television station interviewed them live. They related a sad tale of being robbed—more than eight hundred dollars in American money, and about one hundred bucks Canadian. They had been beaten, they said, when they tried to resist their attacker, and they sported very real bruises and black eyes to show for it. Before the next commercial had aired, hundreds of dollars in donations poured in from big-hearted Canadians with pity on two poor tourists from Minnesota.

Then came a live call from a man who claimed to be the "brute" who had beaten up Beavis and Butthead. His version was a little different. According to our caller, he purchased from the pair some drugs that turned out to be bogus. When he confronted them to demand his money back, they tried to knock him down and flee. That's when the scuffle ensued. Now the news anchor returns live to the remote crew, still with the numbnuts. They, of course, deny the "crazy story concocted by the caller."

Within an hour, the Royal Canadian Mounted Police had linked the men to two break-ins and one robbery through their fingerprints and stolen items on their persons. They both had arrest records for arson, robbery, and petty theft. No matter, they continued to act the part of the Indignant Americans Abroad, complaining all the way to the border and their trial in Minnesota.

Stubborn stooges, eh?

93 Accidental Confession

When Steve Hale was a law officer in Murray, Kentucky, back in the seventies, he received a call at two o'clock in the morning. A motorist reported a car weaving down the road.

Officer Hale found the vehicle within moments and popped on his lights. The car pulled over quickly, if somewhat awkwardly, onto the shoulder of the road. Hale approached the vehicle and explained to the driver he was about to receive a citation for reckless driving.

"I'm normally a really good driver, but I had a lot to drink. I'm really drunk," the guy admitted.

The man's confession certainly simplified things for Hale. All he had to do now was call for backup, go to a judge's house to get a warrant, and return to put the man under arrest.

When court time rolled around the next day, however, the motorist and his attorney had changed the tune. The motorist was willing to plead guilty to reckless driving, but he pled not guilty to driving under the influence. The judge pointed out to the motorist that Hale's report clearly stated the man had admitted being drunk when he was arrested.

Ah, but the motorist had a very good explanation for that. "Your honor, you can't hold that statement against me. When I said that, I was drunk, so it doesn't count."

Case closed.

No, Really, Just Ignore the Facts

Every town has a police impound lot. Your car gets towed there for illegal parking. It's also where the police store confiscated cars used in the commission of a crime.

It stands to reason, if someone dumb left drugs in his impounded car, he might go to check on them at the impound lot—as one young man did in Everett, Washington.

Officer Ybara of the Everett Police Department was cruising his downtown beat when he noticed the young man crouched down between two impounded cars. After a loud warning from Officer Ybara, the young gent stood up.

Ybara patiently waited through the lame excuses that came his way, but none of them warranted breaking and entering. The officer booked the young trespasser, although in less than an hour the guy had made bail. Officer Ybara was heading back out on patrol, so he gave the wise guy a ride back to his car, parked near the impound lot. When they arrived, the smartie got awfully anxious. The officer asked him what was wrong.

"Could you help me get my car open?" the young man asked. "See, I, uh, accidentally locked my keys in the car."

This master criminal had locked his keys in his get-away car.

Shore Loser

Ray Russell is a magistrate in Norfolk, Virginia, and, yes, he has heard them all—that now includes this tale of woe from three sailors singing the bellbottom blues.

This trio of the navy's finest hit port, ready for shore leave. They wasted no time purchasing the necessary libations. The next stop was a deluxe motel room. Within moments, they were on the phone looking for love. That's when they heard a knock on the door.

The three happy sailors were face-to-face with three crooks, all holding guns. The three new arrivals demanded that the sailors hand over everything—money, booze, watches, and wallets. The sailors obeyed the orders begrudgingly, but one just had to protest.

"Don't take our wallets, guys. You don't need our driver's licenses and military IDs. Can't you just take the money and leave the wallets?"

The crooks ignored him. Still, this sailor was adamant. He kept pleading for his wallet. Finally, just as the crooks were ready to make their exit, one of them took mercy on the whiner. He reached into his jacket and threw him the wallet.

He made one sailor very grateful. No, he made all three sailors very, very grateful. You see, the crook had just tossed the sailors his own wallet, complete with driver's license and his parole officer's number.

Their ship had come in, and now it was time for these other three guys to sink all the way to the bottom of a cozy cell.

Nice Pry

Now here's a guy who gets ten points for best comeback—and four years for burglary.

It all began when retired security guard Chris Hughes of Columbia, Tennessee, responded to a silent alarm at one of the warehouses he was hired to patrol. When Officer Hughes arrived at the building, he saw a man with a crowbar, prying on the large overhead door.

"Hey, partner, what are you doin'?" Officer Hughes asked.

The man nearly jumped out of his shoes. "Me? I . . . uh . . . well," he stammered, "well, I'm trying to straighten out this bend in my crowbar!"

The man was arrested, convicted, and given three years for burglary and a fourth for possession of burglary tools. Plenty of time to get things straightened out.

"Me? I . . . uh . . . well," he stammered, "well, I'm trying to straighten out this bend in my crowbar!"

# A Three-Time Loser

Wayne Wilson was working the evening shift for the Peoria, Arizona, Police Department, when he took a call about a robbery in progress at a parked vehicle in a residential neighborhood.

Wilson rolled on it, and he was at the scene in less than two minutes. A young man had been robbed while getting into his car. Luckily, his dad saw the whole thing and called the police. The robber left on foot, headed east.

Moments later, a second squad car pulled up, the suspect in custody. He was fully clothed except for shoes. He was walking in his stocking feet when the officers picked him up. The sock-footed suspect denied any knowledge of the robbery, even though the victim's wallet and watch were in his pants pocket.

One of the backup officers found the thief's getaway car parked two blocks away. In the car were a pair of shoes that fit the thief perfectly. Still, this guy denied any involvement.

Wilson booked him, but within a few hours the suspect made bail and walked out a free man. The very next night, Wilson got a burglary alarm call at a house in that same neighborhood. When he was still a block away, he spotted his shoeless friend from the previous evening walking down the street, stereo in hand. Wilson grabbed him and took him along to the house that had been robbed three doors down the street. Again, the suspect denied any knowledge of a robbery, the whole time clutching a stolen stereo.

The family returned home just as Wilson and the suspect pulled into their driveway. They identified the stereo as theirs, and they pointed out a yellow piece of paper on the garage floor. Wilson picked it up and chuckled as he read aloud the thief's booking report from the evening before. He had dropped it in the house he was robbing.

The court made pretty quick work of the open-and-shut case, and Clueless Shoeless Joe was put away for five to ten. But Wilson advises us that two years later, the same guy was free for all of two days before Wilson arrested him again, this time at the scene of the crime, and, again, with the goods on him and a ready-made denial.

Half Empty or Half Full?

Two men apparently ran out of gas in their pickup truck on a highway outside Laramie, Wyoming. They walked for help. As fate would have it, the first place they came upon happened to be a police station. That wouldn't have been such a bad thing . . . had they not been driving a stolen vehicle. The two were arrested and charged with grand theft auto.

As it turns out, the stolen truck came equipped with two gas tanks. When they ran out of gas on the first tank, anyone else would have flipped a switch to the other tank—which was full.

A Hole in One ... Head

A man working at a golf discount store in Cookeville, Tennessee, was confronted by a man and a woman, who pulled a gun and demanded money. A struggle ensued. The clerk managed to get the gun away from one of the robbers, and he ran from the store with it.

A report was made and a description of the couple given to authorities. The weapon was taken to the station and booked as evidence. An hour later, a nervous woman phoned police to report her gun had been stolen from her motel room.

When Officer Doug Jones arrived at the motel to take the woman's statement, he was greeted by the woman and her boyfriend—who just happened to fit the description of the two golf store robbers. They were arrested and positively identified as the couple in the shop.

Apparently fearful that the weapon could be traced back to her, the woman thought it best to call the police and report the gun stolen.

Eau de Dope

A police officer in steamy Peoria, Arizona, pulled his squad car up to a convenience store to grab a cold soda. Inside he noticed a young man in an aisle near the cashier's line, who appeared to get awfully nervous when he saw the officer.

The cop kept his eye on him and saw Nervous Purvis make eye contact with another young man, who was in line. The guy in line put his hand into his pocket and Nervous quickly left the store.

The cop snagged his soda out of the cooler, and he got into the cashier's line right behind the guy with his hand in his pocket. One whiff of this guy told the officer he must have bought his cologne south of the border. The guy reeked of marijuana. As the toker paid for his chewing gum, the officer had to ask, "Do you have any more dope?"

Without hesitating, the reeking reefer head responded, "No, we smoked it all earlier." The officer paid for his soda, then escorted the bungling bonger outside and called for backup. His buddy Nervous was waiting in a parked car. A subsequent search of the vehicle netted a quantity of marijuana and a stickup note. Say, that cologne really did the trick.